101 SOLUTIONS

TO PROBLEMS IN 401(k) COMMUNICATIONS & EDUCATION

FROM PLAN ADMINISTRATORS NATIONWIDE

INVESTORS
PRESS

Published in the United States by Investors Press, Inc.

Library of Congress Cataloging-in-Publication Data
    Investors Press, Inc.
    101 Solutions To Problems In 401(k) Communications & Education
    From Plan Administrators Nationwide
        ISBN 1-885123-08-6

Printed in U.S.A.

10   9   8   7   6   5   4   3   2   1

Book and jacket design by Silver Communications Inc.

ACKNOWLEDGEMENT

101 Solutions To Problems In 401(k) Communications & Education From Plan Administrators Nationwide is the third Investors Press Guide for 401(k) Administrators. Each Guide in this special Defined Contribution Series examines issues of compelling concern to those responsible for managing and administering their organization's 401(k) plan. A compendium of leading-edge 401(k) thinking, each book in the Series is an easy-to-use, practical guide and an informative, continuing reference resource.

Investors Press acknowledges with appreciation the immeasurable help and cooperation it received in the research and preparation of **101 Solutions.** Special thanks go to those plan administrators who contributed so candidly to the presentation of their company's case study and the following plan sponsors, providers and consultants whose generosity in sharing their experiences, ideas and insights contributed to making this book a valuable resource for plan administrators nationwide.

A.T. Kearney, Inc.
ABM Industries, Inc.
Acme Metals, Inc.
Advanced Micro Devices, Inc.
Air Products & Chemicals
Aluminum Company of America
Amdahl Corp.
American Appraisal Associates, Inc.
American Society of Composers
   And Producers (ASCAP)
American Stores Company
Ampex Corporation
Aon Corporation
Apple Computer
APV Consolidated, Inc.
Arvin Industries, Inc.
Atlanta Gas Light Co.
Baker & McKenzie
BEI Electronics, Inc.
Bellcore
BellSouth Corporation
Blue Cross & Blue Shield of Georgia, Inc.
Blue Cross Blue Shield of Michigan

Blue Shield of California
Briggs & Stratton Corporation
The Homer D. Bronson Company
Calspan SRL Corporation
Chapman and Cutler
The Chronicle Publishing Company
Cincinnati Milacron, Inc.
The Coca-Cola Company
Coca-Cola Enterprises, Inc.
Colonial Pipeline Company
Consolidated Communications, Inc.
Coors Brewing Company
Cox Enterprises, Inc.
CTS Corp.
Duke Power Company
Electrolux Corporation
Energen Corporation
Federal-Mogul Corporation
Fireman's Fund Insurance Co.
Flagstar Corporation
Follett Corp.
Fort Howard Corporation
Fujitsu America, Inc.

Gap, Inc.
GATX Corporation
Genuine Parts Company
Georgia Gulf Corporation
Georgia-Pacific Corporation
GLS Corporation
Great Western Financial Corporation
John H. Harland Co.
Heller, Ehrman, White & McAuliffe
Homestake Mining Co.
Household International Inc.
IBM Corp.
Illinois Department of Central Management
Illinois Power Company
Intel Corporation
J.A. Jones Construction Co.
J.P. Morgan & Co., Inc.
Kendall Packaging Corp.
Lake Region Clinic
Law Engineering & Environmental
    Services, Inc.
Levi Strauss & Co.
LSI Logic Corporation
M.A. Hanna Company
Madison Gas and Electric Company
Michelin North America, Inc.
Michigan Department of Civil Service
Microchip Technology Inc.
Milliken & Company
Morton International, Inc.
Motorola, Inc.
Nike, Inc.
Northern Telecom, Inc.
NYNEX
Oracle Systems Corporation
Pacific Gas and Electric Company
Pacific Telesis Group
PHS, Inc.
Pillsbury Madison & Sutro
Plantation Pipe Line Company
Qualex Inc.
R.R. Donnelley & Sons Co., Inc.
Raychem Corp.
Rayovac Corporation
Riverwood International Corporation
Safeway, Inc.

San Francisco Federal Savings
    and Loan Assocation
Sara Lee Corp.
Sargent & Lundy L.L.C.
SaveMart Supermarkets
SCI Systems, Inc.
Science Applications International
    Corporation (SAIC)
Scientific-Atlanta, Inc.
Seagate Technology, Inc.
Shuttleworth, Inc.
Siliconix, Inc.
Skidmore Owings & Merrill LLP
Sleepeck Printing Company
Springs Window Fashions Division,
    Springs Industries
The Southern Company
Southwire Company
Sterile Concepts, Inc.
Stone Container
The Stroh Brewery Company
Sun Microsystems, Inc.
Tandem Computers Inc.
Thiele Kaolin Co.
Tosco Corporation
TRINOVA Corp.
TRW Investment Management
Turner Broadcasting System, Inc.
University of Pennsylvania
USG Corporation
USL Capital Corp.
Vulcan Materials Company
Westinghouse Savannah River Co.
WICOR, Inc.
Willis Corroon Corp.

American Express Financial Advisors Inc.
Bankers Trust Company
CIGNA Retirement & Investment Services
Delaware Investment & Retirement
    Services, Inc.
Diversified Investment Advisors
Fidelity Investments
John Hancock Funds
Hazlehurst & Associates, Inc.
KeyCorp

101 Solutions To Problems In 401(k) Communications & Education is underwritten by a distinguished group of providers from across the country to whom special appreciation goes from everyone who values the importance of education and the candid exchange of information. Their commitment makes this Guide available to you—the men and women who are charged with meeting the increasingly complex daily challenges of helping your employees achieve retirement security.

INVESTORS
PRESS

101 SOLUTIONS

TO PROBLEMS IN 401(k) COMMUNICATIONS & EDUCATION

FROM PLAN ADMINISTRATORS NATIONWIDE

Underwritten by

AMERICAN EXPRESS FINANCIAL ADVISORS INC.

DIVERSIFIED INVESTMENT ADVISORS

FIDELITY INVESTMENTS®

JOHN HANCOCK FUNDS

KEYCORP

METLIFE

NATIONSBANK

NEUBERGER&BERMAN MANAGEMENT INC.

NYL BENEFIT SERVICES COMPANY, INC.

PRUDENTIAL RETIREMENT SERVICES

ROGERS, CASEY & ASSOCIATES, INC.

STRONG FUNDS

T. ROWE PRICE ASSOCIATES, INC.

UAM RETIREMENT PLAN SERVICES
A SUBSIDIARY OF UNITED ASSET MANAGEMENT CORPORATION (UAM)

THE VANGUARD GROUP

TABLE OF CONTENTS

INTRODUCTION

Although many 401(k) plans can boast of close to 100% participation, enrollment numbers alone do not add up to the real success of a plan. While the importance of joining the plan cannot be minimized, participants must also be educated to save as much as they can as early as they can and to diversify their investments across various asset classes. Despite the best efforts of plan administrators, however, many 401(k) participants do not make the maximum allowable contribution to the plan or match their asset allocation to their retirement time horizons and long-term financial needs.

Industry professionals agree that solutions to important problems like these can be found when peers who confront similar challenges share information and experiences. **101 Solutions To Problems In 401(k) Communications & Education** is a compendium of tools developed by the trailblazers who meet the challenges of daily 401(k) plan administration. These are proven solutions that work: they help employees join, understand and use their 401(k) plans.

The first half of this Guide chronicles the success stories of ten very different plans and describes the obstacles they faced along the way. These case studies compare and contrast the communications and education problems solved by service and manufacturing companies big and small, national and international. Their plan administrators explain the techniques they use to change participant investment behavior and boost contribution levels, increase diversification of 401(k) assets and educate participants and eligible enrollees on how to plan and prepare for a more secure financial future.

The second half continues the Guide's unique peer-to-peer dialogue in a Special Section that lists 101 tips from the trenches, a cross-section of the nation's best thinking from plan administrators and those providers who actively anticipate, understand and meet their growing needs. These tips are bite-sized blocks of clear, concise information, simple solutions and strategies readers can apply quickly and efficiently to solve specific plan management problems and make their 401(k) plan communications and education efforts more successful.

Assembled for the first time in one easy-to-use reference resource, **101 Solutions To Problems In 401(k) Communications & Education** is, literally, an arsenal of both tactical and strategic weapons that can help plan administrators design, develop and implement their own programs.

Tips from the Trenches will be an ongoing resource for plan administrators through the Investors Press Internet Web site, www.investorspress.com and will be updated regularly to offer current, cutting-edge industry thinking.

We invite you to join these innovative trailblazers and share with your peers your insights on how to solve these compelling problems in 401(k) communications and education. Colleagues can borrow from your best thinking and recast your experiences to suit their own particular needs. Please E-mail your own *tips from the trenches* to us at fred@nai.net.

Kathryn A. Sollmann
Managing Editor
Investors Press

CHAPTER ONE

THIS IS NOT A RECORDING:
WORLD-CLASS VOICE RESPONSE

Aluminum Company of America (Alcoa)
Pittsburgh, PA

Alcoa, a corporation whose employee population makes it as large as many cities and as diverse as many countries, boasts 401(k) participation rates that many smaller companies can envy—especially since they were achieved and have been sustained during hectic periods of reorganization that brought thousands of new participants into the plan.

Understanding the peculiarities of a huge manufacturing business ultimately led Alcoa to a telephone voice response system that Sue Burton, administrator of the company's capital accumulation plans, says "is as paperless as we can get it." The success story of how and why Alcoa chose this solution offers ideas and answers that can be useful to plans of any size.

Unions represent about half of Alcoa's U.S. workforce. Although the company's 401(k) plan for salaried employees dates back to 1958, it was not until 1986 that a large majority of union workers voted to participate in a 401(k). Since 1993, most subsidiary, salaried and hourly employees have been offered identical plan features, with the only exception the level of company match.

> - World's leading producer of aluminum for consumer and industrial purposes
> - 64,000 employees in 23 business units
> - 170 locations in 28 countries
> - 34,000 U.S. employees eligible for DC plan
> - 401(k) participation averages 87%
> - Company match varies from 10 cents to $1 on the dollar
> - 401(k) plan assets: $1.5 billion

The initial union plan did not include a company match contribution that could trigger an immediate increase in participation. As it became increasingly clear that Social Security and pensions alone would not ensure a comfortable retirement, Alcoa's challenge was to get its employees involved in planning and providing for their own retirement. Saddled by enormous amounts of paperwork, the company felt that over the long-term it would have to make cost-effective changes in order to do more than merely distribute written materials about saving for retirement.

KIOSKS: A BAND-AID SOLUTION

After reviewing the communications and education options available in 1988, Alcoa installed a computer-based, touch-screen system of kiosks and set them up at Alcoa's U.S. locations to give employees the opportunity to learn about the program, enroll, do retirement modeling and switch investments. "Now many companies have kiosks but back then, that was really something," Burton says.

But even with the kiosks, the flood of paperwork continued as the majority of transactions was still handled by employees' submitting forms. Burton acknowledges that processing all that paper also meant that a lot of time was spent investigating and correcting errors employees made when they filled out the forms.

As a stand-alone system, the kiosks did not meet the needs of all the savings plan participants. Alcoa wanted equal access for every employee and, for a variety of reasons, employees could not access the system through their desktop computers.

"Our population has about 16,000 bargaining people, many of whom do not have computers at work," Burton explains. "Some of our plants are several miles long and although big locations may have two kiosks, that is still inconvenient. Only one person can be on it at a time and it might be very far from an employee's work area. It can take a while to get to, use and get back to where the worker needs to be. In addition, the kiosks were only available during work hours and at plant sites, and were useless to retirees. Compared to accessing information by simply using a telephone, they were expensive, making a wide application of the system unrealistic."

Burton hopes that eventually technology will be able to put that kiosk-based system onto television sets, making it equally available to everyone at home. In the meantime, although an imperfect "stand alone" solution, the kiosks are still available at many locations and are well-utilized as part of a bigger solution—particularly for retirement modeling.

VOICE RESPONSE: AN ONGOING SOLUTION

Alcoa decided to outsource and consolidate the savings plan packages of its many businesses, bringing into one 401(k) program as many as ten separate plans. Burton says the objectives were simplicity and cost containment, plus increased service. The consolidation took a year of work and went into effect in January 1993.

Simultaneously, Alcoa instituted a telephone voice response system which was designed and installed by the same recordkeeper that had provided the computer kiosks. It started in early 1993, as well. "One thing we especially wanted to do was provide consistency across the system so employees would always get the same answers," Burton says. "We wanted to achieve cost efficiencies and provide world-class delivery mechanisms, such as voice response, that are transactional." Employee focus groups had also requested daily prices of their investments.

An 800-number telephone service with voice response seemed to meet all the requirements for easy access that would allow employees to help themselves and relieve much of the administrative burden through automated enrollment and investment selection. Employees could use the system from home, on weekends, whenever they wanted—and it was equally accessible to factory workers, corporate managers and retirees.

These numbers speak volumes.

Over 90% of all rated T. Rowe Price domestic equity funds earned overall ratings of 4 or 5 stars from Morningstar.†

Credit the T. Rowe Price philosophy. It's about investment management that balances risk against return to deliver consistently strong performance over the long run.

And it's about client satisfaction that led to a #1 ranking in two leading national surveys.††

Take a hard look at your 401(k) plan, and consider whether your provider can deliver this kind of strength across the board. Then take an even harder look at T. Rowe Price. We'll be happy to send you the numbers. All you have to do is dial this one: Rick Rockwell (410) 581-5900.

All funds were rated for the 1-, 3-, 5-, and 10-year periods ended 6/30/96, among 2,882; 1,583; 997; and 539 equity funds or 5,076; 2,848; 1,696; and 827 hybrid funds.

Invest With Confidence®

T. Rowe Price
RETIREMENT PLAN SERVICES

Equity funds with 1-, 3-year, and overall ratings: Blue Chip Growth 5, 5, 5; Dividend Growth 5, 5, 5; Mid-Cap Growth 5, 5, 5. Funds with 1-, 3-, 5-year, and overall ratings: Equity Index 5, 4, 4, 4; Science & Technology 3, 5, 5, 5; Small-Cap Value 3, 4, 5, 5; Spectrum Growth 4, 5, 4, 4. Funds with 1-, 3-, 5-, 10-year, and overall ratings: Capital Appreciation 3, 4, 4, 5, 5; Equity Income 5, 5, 5, 5, 5; Growth & Income 4, 4, 4, 3, 4; Growth Stock 4, 4, 4, 3, 4; New America Growth 5, 5, 4, 4, 4; New Era 2, 3, 2, 3, 3; New Horizons 5, 5, 5, 3, 4; *OTC 4, 5, 5, 2, 4. Hybrid fund with 1-, 3-, 5-, 10-year, and overall ratings: *Balanced 4, 4, 4, 4, 4. Six funds have performance records of less than 3 years and, therefore, were not rated. *Performance prior to 9/1/92 reflects investment managers other than T. Rowe Price.

THE EVOLUTION OF VOICE RESPONSE

"Unlike a lot of companies that have only voice response, we went with reps to back it up so that if you're uncomfortable with voice response, or if your question goes beyond the answers you can get through voice response, you can talk to a live person. That has been extremely successful," Burton notes.

She knows, because the company recently completed a series of focus groups at five plants to find out how the telephone system was working. Employees were asked how they would respond if Alcoa expanded the system to include medical and other benefits under one "mega-800-number," as Burton describes it. "Basically the response was—and I wouldn't have believed it if I hadn't heard it myself—'If you do it like the savings plan, we'll be happy.' Some retirees call every day for their account balances, almost like they're calling a broker. We couldn't possibly get live reps to cover all those calls." In one typical month early this year, Burton says, there were nearly 35,000 calls; the plan serves some 26,000 active accounts.

ENSURING SUCCESS

Critical to the system's continuing success has been Alcoa's insistence on staying involved and maintaining an ongoing working relationship with its outside provider. "Once you outsource, keep involved," Burton cautions. "After all these years, we still have weekly status calls. I go there and listen to calls to make sure the responses have an Alcoa feel. Some places outsource and downsize the in-house staff so much there isn't anyone left to monitor the vendor. We take a different approach: we make sure employees get resolution of their problems."

Another critical element in the success of the telephone system, in Burton's opinion, was giving Alcoa's business units no alternative to going paperless. "We had several units say their people could never do this. They wanted to have trans-actions done on paper forms as a back-up or an alternative choice, but we stood fast and said no," Burton explains.

Happily, the skeptics have been proven wrong. Burton says that while some

Just a few of the letters
clients are writing about T. Rowe Price.

Only T. Rowe Price is rated #1 in client satisfaction in both IOMA and Dalbar surveys.[1]

At T. Rowe Price, we never forget it is the clients who write the ratings: #1 overall in client satisfaction and #1 in the key service areas that matter most to clients, from employee education to recordkeeping.

And a #1 rating in investment performance. Credit our philosophy of balancing risk against return for achieving consistently strong results over time.

Take a hard look at your 401(k) plan and consider whether your provider can deliver this level of strength across the board.

Then take a harder look at T. Rowe Price. Just call Rick Rockwell at (410) 581-5900 unless, of course, you'd prefer to write us a letter.

Invest With Confidence®

T. Rowe Price
RETIREMENT PLAN SERVICES

people needed help using the telephone system the first time, they really like the concept. "If you do it well, most folks are not even aware that when they speak to a rep the people they're talking to are not Alcoa employees," she adds.

"Skip the Raise — We'll Take the Match!"

The new system had been operational and earning acceptance for two years when Alcoa's major unions voted for a company match of 401(k) contributions.

Alcoa's policy on matching 401(k) contributions is complicated and, perhaps, unique. It allows each of its business units, and even their sub-units, to determine their own match, depending primarily on their level of profitability and other benefit programs. The match must be calculated on the first 6% of employee pre-tax wages, but Burton says the amount of match varies from 10 cents to dollar-for-dollar.

For example, in 1994 Alcoa's largest bargaining groups voted for a 50 cents-on-the-dollar match instead of a 25 cents-an-hour raise. "In December 1994, before the match went in, 44% of those employees were saving zero," Burton says. "In June 1995, immediately after the match went in, only 24% were saving zero." Participation for all hourly wage workers is now in the high eighties.

Alcoa's matching contribution always starts as company stock. New employees must wait five years before they can move that money into other investments and even longtime employees must leave each year's match in stock for two years before moving it.

Burton believes another factor in Alcoa's high 401(k) participation rate is the company policy of immediate eligibility for new employees. "If you make employees wait, they don't get into the habit of having that money come out of their paychecks," she says. Names of new hires entered in the company's computer system are forwarded to the provider, who then immediately sends out benefit enrollment kits.

Prior to the union vote on whether to choose the 50 cents-on-the-dollar match or a 25 cents-an-hour wage hike, Burton says the company launched a re-education program. Alcoa's most effective tool was a flyer with a picture of a dollar bill on the cover and, pasted on top, a shiny new 50 cent piece: 50 cents "on" the dollar. The flyer listed ten reasons to save and included a brief summary of the investment choices. "Even for the person who didn't 'get the message' from lots of written materials, this was a conversation piece. And we mailed it to employees' homes — we've always found that's the best method. Often, it's the spouse who's won over."

Union members were invited to educational meetings and received Alcoa's regular investment education materials, starting with a very basic investment guide that explains what stocks and bonds are, and progressing to simple examples of how 30-year-old Joe or 60-year-old Phil might invest their 401(k) money. It includes single-page outlines of each fund offered in the plan; in addition to the fixed-income fund and the Alcoa stock fund, the choices are balanced, global, growth or growth and income.

Each quarter, Alcoa sends a report to every participant listing the funds' total returns for the year to date, for the last one, three, five and ten years — and the participant's quarterly statement. The report also discusses news developments that might affect their investments and offers a special section on savings tips.

"In response to employee requests, we recently added on-demand statements. Even though participants can get account balances on voice response in as much

When it Comes to Employee Education,
We're in a Class by Ourselves

Effective Ongoing Education at Pillsbury

401(k)

The biggest challenge in ongoing retirement plan education is breaking through the daily "noise" to get key messages to employees.

Pillsbury

Pillsbury focus groups indicated employees didn't always have a clear picture of the role their 401(k) plan played in their retirement benefit package. To differentiate the plan, we introduced a campaign that used humorous and thought-provoking images of the word "401(k)." The campaign presented basic information in small, frequent doses over a six month period. Over time, it served to redefine perceptions of the plan for employees, giving it its own identity as a 401(k) and helping to increase plan participation.

Helping ShopKo Employees Understand Diversification

Asset diversification was a key goal for ShopKo Stores, Inc., with participants often limiting themselves to the income and equity options of their plan.

Asset Diversification

An education campaign called, "You've Got The Power," helped show employees how they could take control of their investment choices through increased diversification.

ShopKo STORES INC.

The campaign proved to be successful as empowered participants diversified their assets across all investment choices.

Every 401(k) plan presents its own unique challenges for employee education. American Express Institutional Services has gone to the head of the class by helping companies provide employees with the information they need to help them successfully meet their goals.

From building awareness of the plan to measuring program effectiveness, American Express Institutional Services provides a comprehensive, disciplined approach to educating your employees. To find out more, call Ward Armstrong at 1-800-437-0600.

AMERICAN EXPRESS ®

Institutional Services

detail as they want—any time, any day—participants still want it in black and white," Burton sighs. "They call in, request an account balance and it is produced that night and mailed to them the next morning. The report contains all their transactions up to what happened that day. "We were concerned about employees abusing the system by requesting a statement every day," Burton acknowledges, "but fortunately that hasn't happened."

WHAT'S NEXT?

The employee focus groups' enthusiastic responses to the 401(k) plan's 800-number have encouraged Alcoa to begin transferring all their benefits communications to the same system, using the same vendor. Burton says they plan to prepare a video that explains the new "mega-800-number"; Alcoa will send a copy to each employee at home in addition to written materials. Also under consideration is the addition of new 401(k) investment options. Burton expects the savings plan to add more funds early in 1997.

"One of the big thrusts for next year is going to be education—what do we do next? The company's diversification rate among funds has improved but we would like to see even more," she notes. What combination of new initiatives will work best for all employees is not obvious. Alcoa is putting everything on the table for consideration, including expanding the kiosk system, utilizing written materials, handing out software, holding seminars.

Burton also observes that "some companies are using an outside firm to give employees financial planning advice. Some require the employees to pay part or all of the cost and even allow them to select the financial planner."

This kind of opportunity may be a possible next step in Alcoa's continuing efforts to respond to its employees' needs as they plan and prepare for a secure financial future.

CHAPTER

TWO

GETTING TO KNOW YOU:
REACHING OUT TO A DIVERSE WORKFORCE

American Stores Company
Salt Lake City, UT

Reaching out to a scattered audience of 44,000 people, keeping them well informed and building their interest in the company's 401(k) plan surely requires some kind of magic. The American Stores brand of magic is a profit-sharing retirement program that the company contributes to whether the employees do or not. But if they do, they get more.

That is not the only unusual feature of the plan. American Stores' philosophy about 401(k) education and communications also sets it apart from other companies. "Our experience defies traditional assumptions which say you can't give detailed, complex information to people in the ranks. I think the presumption that they cannot get their heads into investment information is wrong," says Scott Bergeson, senior vice president of human resources. "We believe that if we deliver the facts, our employees will draw good conclusions."

In another unique twist, American Stores' employees get professional-quality information directly from Morningstar, which rates American Stores' private label investment funds just as its does public mutual funds.

> Owns and operates grocery and drug stores
> 120,000 employees
> 1,650 stores in 26 states
> Profit-sharing plus bonus for 401(k) participants
> 78% participation in 401(k) plan
> 401(k) plan assets: $3.143 billion

PROFIT-SHARING MATCH

American Stores phased out its DB pension plan in 1984 and replaced it with a defined contribution profit-sharing plan that features a 401(k). Bergeson says the company wanted to provide a retirement benefit, but it also wanted to connect people to the company, give them a direct interest in its performance, link profits to retirement values and incent employees to set aside some of their own money. The strategy worked.

"In our judgment, the plan does change behavior, does cause people to view themselves as being linked with the interests of the company," he says. "When we had a DB plan, employees didn't have a clue about how much that plan was worth to them. No one tied it to whether the company was profitable or not."

Employees who work for American Stores for one year full-time, or 1,000 hours part-time, are eligible automatically for profit-sharing and need only designate where their money should be invested and whether that choice includes participation in the 401(k) plan. Every March the company determines the profit it will share and divvies up 75% of that amount among the eligible employees, based on their pay. The remaining 25% is shared by participants as a kind of company match of their own contributions, up to 6% of salary. Bergeson says a typical 401(k) company match is about 40 cents-on-the-dollar plus the profit-sharing of 5 cents to $5\frac{1}{2}$ cents on each dollar of pay. The match portion vests immediately. The profit-sharing portion begins to vest after three years and is fully vested after seven. Any forfeited profit-sharing contributions go back into the pot for the next year.

Although every employee eligible for profit-sharing must designate an investment choice, American Stores does not offer the usual array of mutual funds. It administers its 401(k) plan itself, as if it were a defined benefit plan, hiring outside investment managers in various specialties and a master trustee that acts as the recordkeeper who provides daily valuations and 24-hour telephone service. The current investment options are short maturity, fixed-income, balanced and equity, plus company stock.

"We set the asset allocation mix for those managers, we define the risk characteristics of the specific investment options," Bergeson explains. "We may decide that 25% of the equity component should be in international, then we decide on the three managers who will have that allocation. When participants choose to put money into the balanced fund, they're really getting a piece of several different fixed-income managers and a piece of several equity managers all wrapped up in a single net asset value."

From the employees' viewpoint, the result is indistinguishable from ordinary mutual funds, except that they cannot read about their funds in personal finance magazines or check fund performance in daily newspapers—a situation that presented both a problem and an opportunity. The solution was a biannual Fund Guide the company began publishing some years ago; it goes to every employee at home. In line with the company's philosophy of total disclosure, the Guide broke down the underlying portfolios of every investment manager and listed every security included in each investment option.

"We didn't expect participants to understand all of those securities. We were trying to teach some very basic principles of investing, such as that the two major moderating influences on risk are diversification and time. People need to understand what a diversified portfolio means and how important it is to have one," Bergeson explains. The Guide demonstrated that lesson, but what it did not do was give any comparative assessment of fund performance.

American Stores' management knew its funds were managed by some of the best professionals in the business, but realized that comparing them objectively to public mutual funds could greatly enhance employee confidence and possibly attract even larger contributions and more participants. Last year, Bergeson hired Morningstar to do for the company's funds what it does for public funds.

"With Fidelity's CORPORATEplan, we went from zero to 90% participation. The other 10% are probably hoping to hit the jackpot."

Jessica Wasner, Office Manager, Desktop Data

◆ ◆ ◆ ◆ ◆

Having a great product doesn't mean people will automatically buy it. To accomplish that takes something more. To Desktop Data, a developer of news processing software, that something more was Fidelity's approach to 401(k) plans – an integrated and coordinated service, all under one roof and only available directly from Fidelity.

"From day one, The CORPORATEplan *for Retirement* was great," said Desktop Data's Office Manager, Jessica Wasner. "Getting the plan started was an absolute breeze. I had no idea it would be as easy as it was."

"Fidelity's people were great. They explained everything in simple terms – without talking down to anyone. Of course, their enrollment and communications materials are great, too."

And all that made a difference? "90% participation right off the bat. I'd say, yes, a big difference. Wouldn't you?"

TheCORPORATE*plan*
F O R   R E T I R E M E N T

Your retirement plan. Our full time job.

If you want this level of commitment behind your plan, call Fidelity for a free brochure at 1-800-343-9184. Your retirement plan is our full time job.

Fidelity Investments®

1-800-343-9184 Ext. 7306
Visit us on the Internet at http://www.fid-inv.com

The result is a remarkable booklet that opens with a brief introduction by Bergeson, followed by a two-page User's Guide and full-page analyses and ratings of the American Stores' investment funds, including objectives, performance charts and graphs, asset allocation, risk analysis, portfolio analysis and a written description of each. There is also a full-page analysis of each of the 21 American Stores investment managers. A list breaks down each fund's holdings and describes the company stock. The funds are rated and assigned stars just as the mutual funds are in Morningstar's public reports.

Morningstar has now produced two of these biannual reports for American Stores and both times Bergeson has polled a statistically significant sample of employees using a telephone survey conducted by a professional survey organization. The response to the first guide was positive. "Overall, they liked it. Some said it was too complicated, some were thrilled. Basically we got about half the people to read it," Bergeson says, which was a little better than the response to the company's own Fund Guide. The second report received somewhat more than 50% readership. "As nearly as we can tell, the difference is that we put a more colorful cover on it," Bergeson notes. "That's the only thing we changed. So win one for Madison Avenue."

Whether or not these reports will really change investment behavior may take years to determine. Bergeson says the employee's investment allocation has been holding steady for several years at about 57% in equities and he is quite comfortable with that.

Participation has inched up slightly over the last few years, but 75% is better than it sounds. Out of the total 44,000 participating employees, only about 33,000 are making contributions to the 401(k) plan, and that number remains quite constant. Bergeson believes he is already succeeding in reaching almost all his potential participants. "Is it reasonable to expect we're going to get a person who's 21 years old, working part-time and going to school? Probably not," he believes.

"Before Fidelity's CORPORATEplan, I didn't know who to call if things went wrong with our 401(k). Now that I do know, nothing goes wrong."

Joe Rokus, Vice President, Finance & Chief Financial Officer, GALILEO ELECTRO-OPTICS

◆ ◆ ◆ ◆ ◆

GALILEO began their 401(k) plan with a promising thought. Pick experts for each aspect of the plan and everything should fall into place. The problem is, the more players you have involved, the more that can potentially go wrong.

"We had a plan administrator in one place and a recordkeeper in another. And when something went wrong, there was never any accountability. It was time for a change."

GALILEO reviewed nearly ten leading 401(k) providers and, ultimately, selected The CORPORATEplan *for Retirement*℠– a coordinated service, all under one roof and only available directly from Fidelity. And it's designed exclusively for small to mid-sized companies.

"They turned what used to be a nightmare into a dream."

"Now statements are accurate and on time," said Rokus. "And it's a major relief knowing that when I call, I'll get action. I almost wish something would go wrong. Well, not really."

If you want this level of commitment behind your plan, call for Fidelity's CORPORATEplan *for Retirement* brochure at 1-800-343-9184. Your retirement plan is our full time job.

Your retirement plan. Our full time job.

Call or write for our brochure: Fidelity Investments®
200 Magellan Way, Covington, KY 41015, Attn: Charles Carrico

Name_____	Title_____
Company_____	
Address_____	
City_____	State_____ Zip_____
Phone_____	Fax_____

It explains why we're the one choice for small to mid-sized companies.

1-800-343-9184 Ext. 7306
Visit us on the Internet at http://www.fid-inv.com

REACHING OUT TO EMPLOYEES

That does not mean that he doesn't try. Just maintaining present participation and diversification rates requires constant effort. American Stores reaches out to its diverse workforce of young, old, part-time, full-time, stable, mobile employees with every tool it can put to good use. In addition to the professional Fund Guides, written materials include quarterly reports and account statements that are sent to each participant at home. Bergeson puts posters and table-tents in the stores' lunchrooms that focus on a different topic each quarter, such as the value of compound interest or the benefit of saving early in life.

The core of the program is an annual meeting at each store scheduled immediately after the company profit-sharing and 401(k) contributions are distributed. These meetings are led by the store managers, each of whom receives from headquarters "meeting-leader" guides that tell them exactly what to do, as well as a series of flip-charts and a 10- or 12-minute video. Each year the materials feature a particular educational theme, such as risk versus return, the importance of personal contributions to the 401(k) plan or how easy it is to get a loan from the plan.

"We think that one of the big barriers to getting younger people to contribute to the plan is their concern about how to deal with emergencies. They worry about being able to get their hands on that money," Bergeson says. "If they know they can initiate a loan and have access to their money, that barrier is weakened."

Bergeson believes the most important communications tool he has now is the 800-number voice response system initiated in 1992. It gets as many as 65,000 calls a month; 50,000 callers use voice response and the others talk to a service rep. "We think this is a vital communications tool because people have a heightened sense of self-confidence when they know they have access to information and the ability to make a decision or a change."

Having experimented with targeted marketing to non-contributors and low contributors, he likes the results and may do more. "They've just been little reminders but they've triggered some activity. A card that says, 'This year people who made personal contributions made 40 cents on every dollar and we just wondered why you weren't doing that too...' has a powerful impact when a spouse gets a hold of it," he says. "We call it free money—we just let them know they're missing out on free money."

KNOW YOUR 401(k) CUSTOMER

Every year after the annual meeting, the company conducts a survey to measure the effectiveness of its communications and quickly applies the lessons it learns. "We've shortened our print materials. We used to have a 12-page annual report on the 401(k); now it's a four-page brochure. We've discovered that people don't want to hear a lot of training in the videos about how the plan works. People who are already in the plan get turned off by introductory information, so we've created a separate video to train new people," Bergeson explains.

These surveys indicate a high level of satisfaction with the investment options and the 401(k) plan structure, but Bergeson says they also suggest interest in having additional investment options. "Some participants may wish to take additional risk or have more international exposure, so clearly some of them have a better

Of all the places people choose for their retirement, this is one of the most popular.

As one of the nation's largest institutional investment managers, there isn't a more desirable place for your company's 401(k) plan than Prudential. Fifty million customers worldwide trust us for financial and employee benefit services, which goes a long way toward increasing employee participation in your retirement plan.

With more than $224 billion in assets under management, Prudential is one of the nation's largest investment managers.

Of course, employee acceptance alone doesn't account for $36 billion in defined contribution assets. That took time; we're in our fourth decade as a DC manager.

Jennison and other specialty managers offer diversification and institutional investment management expertise.

It took investment experience, as exemplified by our institutional investment managers, such as Jennison Associates. And it took innovation in recordkeeping, like an imaging system that gives service reps on-line access to every piece of correspondence in a participant's file – originals,

Over 50 million customers worldwide trust The Rock to help them reach their goals.

within seconds. All of which makes the journey to retirement smoother for everybody, and Prudential a comfortable place to retire indeed. For a free brochure on The Prudential 401(k) plan, contact your Prudential representative or give us a call at 1-800-862-3344 today. **The Prudential 401(k)**

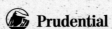 **Prudential**

understanding of various alternatives they might select as they allocate their money," he says. "In my view, developing a tolerance among plan participants to market variables is one of the really serious challenges facing the plan sponsor."

The surveys have produced another intriguing finding that seems to demonstrate the limits of what corporate communications can achieve: a decision to contribute to a 401(k) plan usually involves an important other person. "Very often it's a spouse," Bergeson notes. "Sometimes it's a peer at the work site, and that's probably more valuable and exerts more influence on the initial decision to defer or increase the deferral than all the communications we do. If you can get people to talk about the plan with a spouse or a fellow worker who has a favorable view, that really has a tremendous impact."

Consequently, the company's most recent video showed a lot of happy employees extolling the benefits of putting money into the 401(k) plan. That is the kind of communications program Bergeson believes in: a responsive, sustained process of change and improvement. Aside from considering new investment options, he expects the future to be more of the same—a constant battle against investment and retirement planning inertia using any new tool that seems promising. "We're open to thinking about all the possibilities available in the marketplace," he promises.

BYTES OF THE APPLE:
INFORMATION DELIVERY ON THE WEB

Apple Computer
Cupertino, CA

Dream and reality collided happily at Apple Computer during the spring of 1996 when the company implemented a long-planned program to transfer all of its employee benefit information to an internal web site cross-linked to the mutual funds in its 401(k) plan, its medical insurer and other key service providers.

The new web site gives employees access to a wide range of human resources information, including anything they might want or need, for example, on training and career development and employee policies and practices. As an important feature, it includes every form employees need to sign up for benefits, take out a loan or get reimbursed for expenses. "It has over a thousand documents. It's huge," observes Sally Brewster, Apple Benefits Manager and the dreamer who envisaged a better, more user-friendly system than the collection of software applications and E-mail bulletin board communications Apple installed in 1990. "Those materials worked fine for six years and from talking to other people I know we were way ahead of most companies. But we always want to do it better," she says.

> ➤ Designs and manufactures computer hardware and systems software
>
> ➤ 9,540 employees
>
> ➤ 85%–90% 401(k) participation
>
> ➤ Tenure-based, graduated company match up to 6% of salary
>
> ➤ 401(k) plan assets: $350 million

THE SYSTEM APPLE OUTGREW

Apple's original collection of electronic tools and documents included Mac 401(k), an application which utilized HyperCard®, an information management system that was shipped with every Macintosh. Employees used it to enroll in the 401(k) plan and get the information and explanations they needed about the company's matching contribution, tax advantages, mutual fund choices, daily valuations, personal savings and retirement projections. Mac 401(k) offered modeling and projected what various contribution levels—as a percentage of an employee's salary—would generate after five, ten or fifteen years, assuming a given interest rate. To help with retirement planning, it had Social Security tables built in, made allowances for personal savings and showed how they all added up.

"For our administrative purposes, all we really needed was the enrollment part, but we wanted it to be an educational tool as well because this is our only pension plan," Brewster explains. "We figured that when employees are enrolling, that's the moment we have their mindshare so let's put it right there and then they can do the modeling and see that instead of 6% maybe they had better put in 10%. That was the ulterior motive."

The entire package was posted on Apple's E-mail system along with hundreds of other documents, forms and information, making it equally accessible to employees in any of Apple's more than 30 locations from sales offices to factory floors. Although sophisticated and thorough, the E-mail bulletin board was stuffed with so much information that navigating it could be cumbersome and frustrating. Information was arranged hierarchically: in order to change their 401(k) contribution, for instance, employees had to go into E-mail, click on 401(k), open one folder and then another to find what they wanted. If what they wanted wasn't there, they had to back out and try another set of folders. When they finally found what they needed, Mac 401(k) had to download it to a desktop computer before they could use the software to fill out the form or print out the information they needed.

Unfortunately, there was no technology available at that time that could improve the system. Brewster wanted it to hold a great deal of information, allow quick and easy access to any document or index, link up with electronic forms—enrollment, address changes, expenses, etc.—and still be easy and intuitive for people to use.

"I and a couple of other people here at Apple have had this vision for a long time, so we've been watching the marketplace very carefully. I've looked at so many demonstrations of different products!" Brewster exclaims. They considered various software tools that became available—groupware and benefit consultants' programs—but none was right. They wanted applications software as well-designed and easy to use as the operational systems that have made Apple famous, but they had to wait for someone else to solve the problem because this type of applications software is not Apple's business.

Brewster paid close attention when the new Web browser software began to appear more than a year ago. "It was starting to look promising and I thought about using it for open enrollment," she explains. "I talked to our information systems people and said, 'This is what I'm thinking about. What do you think?' They told me they were looking at the same idea for the entire company network, so I was on the right track and should go for it. It was really my side coming together with the technology when it was ready."

PUSHING THE TECHNOLOGY ENVELOPE

Various human resource department groups, including employee benefits and information, were able to design their own Web pages within a loose structure created by Apple's information systems department to carry the entire company network. It took them less than six months to cover the basics. What they wrought has taken several months to put in place, starting in February 1996 with a general employee program and benefits information, and following in April

with open enrollment for benefits that gives employees access to their own personal information.

"What's great about the Web is that you can have a document of text and within the text have words that are highlighted that link to other documents so you can click and go to whatever you want to find out about," observes Brewster happily.

The most radical—and truly innovative—aspect of this technological transformation is that the new web site offers Apple's 401(k) plan participants any and all information about their mutual fund investment options *directly from the mutual fund company itself*. If employees look up investment options and then want to know more about a particular fund, they can click on the fund's name and be zapped over to the fund company's own Web page. There they will find complete information on that fund, including who the fund manager is, fund strategy, long-term performance, daily net asset value, top ten holdings and any other information the investment manager considers important.

Apple's 401(k) plan currently offers seven mutual funds that cover various fixed-income and equity investment styles from one of the major fund families. An important administrative benefit of the Web is that Apple no longer needs to maintain and reproduce all that fund information in order to make it easily accessible to Apple employees: now they can get the fund company's own information directly, whenever they want it, with just an easy click of a mouse. Furthermore, Brewster says all this is cheap: the whole system was done using Macintosh desktop computers, not some mainframe in the basement.

Employees can also click on the word for whatever application form they need and bring it up on their own screen. Enrollment form data goes directly into Apple's database, just as it did with the HyperCard system, but the form is much more accessible on the Web and doesn't have to be downloaded to the user's own desktop. "Any form can be filled out right there on the Web and then sent directly to the benefits department," explains Brewster. "It's really slick."

Apple's employees agree. About 1,900 employees enrolled in the 401(k) via the Web, an impressive number since there were no benefit plan changes during the year and most employees "defaulted" to their prior year plans and did not need to enroll. Almost 70% of those who did enroll via the Web completed the questionnaire at the end of the enrollment form and volunteered comments, such as "This is immensely helpful…it really makes things easier and I feel more secure. I make my choices and then they are reflected back to me instantly. This method of open enrollment can't be beat!" "Great to see HR take this kind of lead!" "This was FUN!" "One of the best uses of technology I have seen at Apple. Excellent job! I look forward to using the service in the future." "I was really impressed with the fact that the data was personalized for me. You've done a great job with this." "Thanks for making it easy for me to enroll. It saves money and time by doing it this way." Really slick, indeed.

All the information, educational exercises and retirement modeling that were part of the old HyperCard system are being transferred directly to Apple's internal web site, but not all the cross-links to service providers are hooked up yet. Brewster notes that any technological problems with the Web itself are now handled in-house by Apple's information systems staff; questions about the 401(k) plan or any benefit continue to be referred to the human resources help-line. Both numbers

> **"MONEY MARKET FUNDS ARE MADE UP OF STOCKS."**
>
> **"THE BEST TIME TO INVEST IN BOND FUNDS IS WHEN INTEREST RATES ARE RISING."**
>
> **"COMPANY STOCK IS LESS RISKY THAN A DIVERSIFIED STOCK FUND."**

John Hancock regularly sponsors independent research like the *Participant Attitudes on Retirement Saving* study conducted by the Gallup Organization. We do this in order to better understand and address information gaps, illustrated by the statements above, among retirement investors.

If misperceptions like these sound all too familiar, your company may need to invest in an educational program that works—with a retirement plan provider that is committed to helping employees learn.

At John Hancock Funds we're dedicated to helping people build a solid foundation of retirement and investment knowledge.

Find out more about the John Hancock Funds' Employee Education and Communication Program and our Plan Participation Guarantee by calling Edward J. Lavelle, First Vice President (617) 375-4706.

Institutional Funds   401(k)   Profit-Sharing
Money Purchase   403(b)   Defined Benefit

 JOHN HANCOCK FUNDS
A Global Investment Management Firm

 John Hancock ®
Financial Services

John Hancock Funds, Inc., 101 Huntington Avenue, Boston, Massachusetts 02199

Boston ■ *New York* ■ *Chicago* ■ *San Francisco* ■ *Los Angeles*

appear at the bottom of every Web page. In fact, instead of having to make a telephone call, anyone can click on the appropriate number, be connected automatically to E-mail and send a message right then and there. Brewster says the Web system is so simple and obvious it does not require any special lessons or training.

The hardest part of designing this remarkable new system proved to be technological—being forced to use HyperText Markup Language (HTML), the standard language used to code documents for the Internet. Brewster describes it as "really awkward". Because software designed to simplify that programming didn't do everything that was needed, the whole process of creating the web site took longer than anticipated. Notwithstanding that one inconvenience, Brewster believes that when all the work is completed the Web will deliver the quick, easy and complete educational information system she dreamed of with no gaps or omissions.

STOCK IT TO ME!

With slightly less than tongue in cheek, Apple's engineers enhanced an existing "just for fun" program called *Stock It To Me!* that allows anyone in the company with a computer terminal to list a number of stocks and/or mutual funds and follow their performance closely. The program updates stock quotes every 15 minutes via a satellite link. "It started out as a simple, kind of crude little thing and then they developed it and enhanced it so now it can be a screen saver. It floats around and you can see the stock prices changing," Brewster explains with a smile. The mutual fund numbers are updated just once a day after net asset values are calculated.

WHY THE WEB?

As much fun as all this is, Brewster says Apple upgraded to an internal web site not because it was possible, but because it made it easier for employees to get the information and help they need. Brewster is a big believer in giving people the information they want when they want it and are receptive to receiving it, whatever time of day or night that might be. Interestingly, she is not counting on the Web for any additional benefits such as increased participation in the plan.

"I hope this makes participating in the 401(k) plan easier," she says. "We'll probably only get incremental increases in participation, but the easier we make it for people, the less of a barrier there will be. If it's fun and entertaining, which the Internet is, then people will think it's neat and they'll play with it and then maybe they'll say, 'I can understand this. I should do this.'"

Apple's workforce of just under 10,000 includes factory employees who manufacture the machines, as well as the wizards who create the famous Apple operating systems. "The people in the manufacturing plants are a challenge because they don't have desks, they don't have computers. They make them, but they don't necessarily use them. We have to work with the human resources people at the sites, who set up rooms with several computers in them so people can come and do their enrollment. They take a little more hand-holding," Brewster observes.

Those computers are available to every employee and may actually give some their only opportunity to use a computer and try out the Internet. The new web site is

so easy to manipulate that Brewster says even those employees who do not use computers regularly are able to navigate through the system without special training. "That's the point of it," she says. "It's literally point and click." She hopes workers will take advantage of the system, but Apple carefully hedges its bet and also uses many other more traditional tools to get its 401(k) communications and education message out.

In addition to the telephone help-lines, there are benefits brochures, targeted mailings to non-participants, employee meetings throughout the year at different sites and brown-bag lunch meetings featuring informal lectures and conversations on financial topics. "We use a wide range of tools and techniques because no one thing works for everybody," Brewster explains. "We especially go after the manufacturing sites and work out a special strategy with the local human resource people so there is plenty of pre-publicity to insure that people are ready for us when we come out for a meeting."

RAISING THE ANTE RAISES PARTICIPATION

Although it is still too early to know if the novelty, ease and accessibility of the web site itself will attract new 401(k) customers, what *has* increased plan participation are increases in the company match. Apple's contribution to an employee's 401(k) is based on length of service; employees are eligible to participate as soon as they start work. The match has ratcheted up in the last several years from 30 cents, 50 cents and 70 cents to a current 50 cents-on-the-dollar for one to two years of employment, 75 cents-on-the-dollar for three to five years and dollar-for-dollar for five years or more, up to 6% of total salary. Brewster achieved the last increase by curbing some particularly rich medical benefits and shifting some of the savings into the 401(k) budget. She notes that participation has risen in tandem with the increases in the company match, from 70% participation before it went to 30-50-70 cents to about 85%–90% now, depending on new hiring levels.

IMMEDIATE CONCERNS

One of Brewster's immediate concerns is keeping all this information private. "We've had a lot of concerns about security and I have had some long, hard conversations with our informations systems people about that. The Apple Web is internal so it's not accessible for someone out on the public Internet, America Online® or whatever. They can't get in and see any of this information." Each employee has a password to access their personal information and a complex security system has been created to allow employees to link up with it from home computers with modems. Keeping private information private remains a high priority.

Other difficult issues created by this high-tech magic include meeting Securities and Exchange Commission disclaimer requirements. Although all the legal qualifiers—such as noting that past performance does not predict future performance—are now the first thing users see on the mutual fund web site, Brewster shares industry concerns that there is nothing to prevent participants from bypassing that introductory information.

"There is nothing that prevents someone from setting a bookmark for a particular fund and just going straight there the next time they use the system and never seeing that legal stuff again. Nor is there anything to prevent us from creating a direct link from our pages straight into their fund pages because that's the very nature of the Web—you can go directly wherever you want, you don't have to go through a hierarchical structure. So we're struggling with how to make sure we meet those legal requirements when we can't control what people do."

Another concern she has is the ability the system offers people to enroll in a mutual fund without receiving the legally required literature. Is putting prospectuses on the Internet an adequate method of delivering that information? "There's a whole bunch of issues like that we're going to have to grapple with as this evolves," Brewster notes.

LOOKING AHEAD: SPINNING A WIDER WEB

The first test of the new web site was Apple's open enrollment in April 1996. "An employee survey is giving us a lot of important feedback. I'm not surprised because our employees are very vocal about telling us what they think." Brewster also relies on the help-lines to find out what bothers employees. "All their calls are logged and we look at the statistics and review what they're about. If there is a higher volume in one area, that's a flag to us that people are confused and we need to do something about it."

Brewster expects the immediate future to be difficult and busy as she and her colleagues complete their Web databases with all its cross-links, and then add some bells and whistles. For a company famed for its graphics, she acknowledges that the new system lacks pizzazz.

"Right now it's not very pretty because it's such a job just to get the content developed—but it will be. We're definitely working on spiffing it up, putting graphics in there, charts, colorful stuff. It's going to keep evolving pretty intensively for at least another year because our providers are developing their stuff, too. It's all just moving so fast."

Apple's Web site cross-links to the public Internet sites of its mutual fund, medical and other service providers, but planned future links will be much more personal.

How Does Vanguard Help You Keep A Step Ahead?

Vanguard is owned by the shareholders of our Funds. Why should our corporate structure be important to 401(k) sponsors and participants?

Because at Vanguard, profits that might otherwise be paid to a management company are used to benefit our clients, to expand our technological leadership in providing superior service, and to maintain the lowest investment costs in the mutual fund industry.

Vanguard Online/ America Online® and Vanguard/ World Wide Web

serve participants who increasingly rely on electronic means to access timely financial news and comprehensive investment information.

Participant Online

is a convenient, private investment education and account information center for retirement plan participants that also offers convenient account transaction processing.

Desktop

heightens the skills of more than 200 Vanguard Associates by enabling them to access multiple screens to efficiently perform a variety of account-related transactions virtually simultaneously and to open special reference windows for complete and accurate answers to questions.

Vanguard VOICE™ Network

is available 24 hours every day for comprehensive telephone service that includes fund and account information and selected transactions, including automated loans and withdrawals.

Desktop Videoconferencing

combines video and audio with document-sharing over digital phone lines to bring participants at remote locations to Vanguard's campus for one-on-one retirement planning counseling.

To keep your organization's retirement program

a step—or two—ahead, call F. William McNabb at 1-800-523-1036, Ext. 4056. Or visit us on America Online at Keyword: Vanguard or on the World Wide Web at http://www.vanguard.com

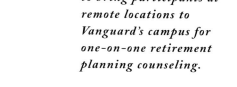

Apple's providers are working on additions that Brewster says will allow employees to access their personal accounts "so someone could log on and actually see their account as of the end of the day." This also means that eventually Apple will not have to produce quarterly statements for its 401(k) plan participants—all that information will be available on the Web from the provider.

Nothing prevents other companies from following in Apple's footsteps and creating their own internal web sites with cross-links to their service providers. Brewster says Apple's providers are already talking to their other clients about implementing some of the same ideas.

"Lots of companies already have networks in place and if they have Macs or PCs, they've already got the hardware. Our internal Web pages are on a bunch of Macs," she explains. "With Web browsers like Netscape or Mosaic, it's really easy to get on the Web. You have to do a one-time installation of the browser, which is like installing any other piece of software on your desktop. If you have that and the communications software, then you're ready to go."

Apple has drawn successfully on both outside resources and internal expertise to develop and refine a system for its employees that delivers easy access to the information they need. Using its company-wide web site in combination with other more traditional educational tools gives Apple a powerful set of strategies that helps it meet the challenge of educating its employees as they plan for a safer and more secure retirement.

CHAPTER FOUR

Pay For Performance:
What's Good For The Company Is Good For You

The Homer D. Bronson Company
Winsted, CT

Pay for performance is the philosophy of The Homer D. Bronson Company these days. Founded in 1839, the company was a dying relic when Henry Martin bought it in 1990 and began its turn-around. By 1995, there was enough money to set up a 401(k) plan as the company's only retirement program. "We did it because our employees had been asking for it and we felt that after medical and dental care and a disability plan, this was the next most important thing we could do for them," Martin explains. "Our philosophy has always been that as the company grows and we continue to turn it around, we want to share with the employees and add back some benefits for them."

> ➤ Designs and manufacturers custom hinges for industry
>
> ➤ 70 employees
>
> ➤ 77% participation in 401(k) plan
>
> ➤ 10%-50% performance-based match, up to 4% of salary
>
> ➤ 401(k) plan assets: $150,000

But Martin also wanted the plan to be an incentive and fit his pay-for-performance philosophy. The question was how. As a privately held business, the only financial data Bronson discloses is sales. Martin values that privacy so a profit-based incentive was not feasible. The challenge was to find another way.

After long deliberations, the decision was made to implement a 401(k) plan with a company match, adjusted every six months within a range of 10% to 50%, up to 4% of salary, depending on the company's performance in achieving four or five strategic goals. Setting those goals initially proved more difficult than expected.

Some of the more obvious objectives—increasing sales by 10%—did not work because they were too narrow. "What does that mean to the guys in shipping?" asks Bronson CFO Walter Schuppe. "They can only ship what's made. What does it mean to production? They can only make what we sell. So it's really only geared to sales."

SETTING GOALS

The company needed broader criteria that would let everyone feel a part of its growth and success. Martin and Schuppe decided initially on three basic guidelines: the goals must be important strategically for the long-term success of the business; they must be easily measurable and communicable; and most employees should be involved in some way, or have some impact on, achieving these goals. Once broad guidelines were established, Martin says it became easy to set specific company-wide goals.

"We always have a safety-oriented goal which we measure through lost work days," Martin explains. Lost work days were high for a while; employees wanted them lowered because they wanted a safe workplace and management wanted them reduced to minimize workmen's compensation costs. It was a shared goal that suited everyone.

Quality is another goal that affects everyone. "We have a quality assurance goal measured by the dollar value of returned goods versus total sales," Martin explains. That covers products returned because they were not billed or shipped properly, or returned as a result of faulty design or production. Maintaining the company's ISO 9000 rating, an international standard of quality that is re-certified each year, is also part of the company's concern for quality. When it's time for the ISO audit, maintaining the certification is another important goal.

"In addition," Martin adds, "we have a marketing goal in each six-month period. We try to penetrate some major account that's new to us—last year it was the Ford Motor Company. We ask ourselves how we did on that: did we make it come in on time, on budget and is the customer happy?" Martin says. There may also be some kind of productivity goal, such as devising ways to cut costs for a major customer.

The goals can change every six months. If a goal is achieved, it's replaced with another one. "We might raise or lower the hurdle on a goal that we haven't achieved or that's ongoing," Martin explains. "At the end of each six-month period, we take a look at the thing from scratch."

PAY FOR PERFORMANCE

Martin claims the biannual calculation that translates those goals into the company's 401(k) matching contribution is not as difficult to determine as it may seem. He and Schuppe devised a simple matrix to accommodate four or five goals that are listed vertically against nine degrees of match that head columns horizontally in increments of 5%, from 10% to 50%.

For the safety goal, as an example, one lost work day might be at the 50% match level; five lost work days might be at the 10% or 15% match level. Each goal gets a score and a simple average is computed that becomes the company match for the next six months. Each goal is considered to have equal value so there is no weighting. "We consider 25% to be par," Schuppe says. "We always set the goals with the idea that we think we can achieve them and, if we do, it will be a 25% match."

Schuppe is not sure that everyone understood the idea the first time it was explained and says that although factory workers are unlikely to ask many questions at company meetings, their questions do eventually float up from the plant floor. Now that the program has been in effect for a while and explained several times, he thinks everyone gets it.

The 401(k) plan was put into effect in January 1995, with 25% as the initial match, based on the prior year's performance. The match increased to 35% after

METLIFE MAKES 401(k) EDUCATION EASY.

At MetLife's Defined Contribution Group, we think easy ongoing education and communication are essential to a successful 401(k) plan.

For example, BenePhone,® our interactive voice response system, includes "Listen and Learn" where participants can get valuable insights on a variety of retirement planning topics. Our experienced retirement service representatives offer more than just customary account information. They also educate and enlighten. So plan participants have access to the accurate, relevant information they need to make confident retirement planning decisions.

For more information on how MetLife can make 401(k) education easy, call us at 1-800-722-6091 or e-mail: info@metlife.com.

EDUCATE-COMMUNICATE

Defined Contribution Group

✳ MetLife®

the first six months, then moved down to 25% at the second assessment. Every six months there is a company-wide meeting at which the new match and performance numbers are reviewed. The 10% to 50% spread was chosen to assure employees that there would always be some match. "Even in a worst-case scenario, it can never go to zero," says Martin.

He believes the most attractive part of the 401(k) plan for employees is not necessarily the match—which he acknowledges does not add up to a significant part of their total compensation—but the tax-deferred benefits. "It does not take a super-high match or a super-high rate of return by the money manager to make such a plan more attractive than any savings account," Martin explains. "Our people appreciated having a retirement plan put into effect for them. It's something that was on their minds a lot."

MAKING CHOICES

The company selected one of the largest mutual fund companies to manage its 401(k). Schuppe says Bronson's small size did not limit the field—plenty of vendors were interested. The company considered seven, then made its choice based on service and price and got a full-service contract that includes handling the entire administrative burden. Schuppe chose the investment options himself, selecting eight funds that cover the gamut of risk: a U.S. Treasury money market for the severely risk-averse, a Ginnie Mae fund, high-yield and high-quality corporate bond funds, balanced, small-cap and two styles of growth funds.

"I tried to pick funds that had good Morningstar ratings, good performance, covered all the different intervals from safety to risk and were not too specialized so the employees couldn't end up inadvertently hurting themselves," Schuppe explains, rejecting for that reason a sector fund that was hot at the moment and requested by a couple of people.

The fund company sent its own people to explain the 401(k) plan and introduce the investment options to Bronson's employees. The company organized two meetings in order to keep them small and give everyone a chance to ask questions. The fund representatives distributed written materials and enrollment forms, discussed saving and investing and explained the difference between safety and risk and the risk/reward trade-off. Schuppe says about 80% of the employees signed up right away and that participation level has remained fairly constant.

Follow-up education in a company this size tends to be personal and on an "as-needed" basis. Schuppe answers questions himself when anyone calls or when he's walking through the plant. He introduces new employees to the plan as part of their initiation. Last summer he conducted an informal sign-up campaign by approaching employees who were not in the plan and explaining the benefits of participation. "That had some success. I picked up two or three more," he says. "And I talked to the people who were already participating and tried to get them to increase their contributions."

Every month he uses company bulletin boards to post graphs of the closing net asset values for each fund, starting from when the plan began. The fund company sends each participant a quarterly statement, accompanied by an investment newsletter, and provides a full-service 800-number to call for information or to change investments. Most transactions are paperless.

ONLY METLIFE GUARANTEES TO INCREASE YOUR 401(k) PLAN PARTICIPATION.

With MetLife's MetAssure,℠ if your plan participation is not reaching the levels we agree upon up front, then we automatically work with you until we meet those levels, at no additional charge.

It's the MetLife Participation Guarantee, and it's just one of the many innovative features you'll find in our acclaimed education and communication process.

For more information on the MetAssure Participation Guarantee or to learn more about our extraordinary education emphasis, call us at 1-800-722-6091 or e-mail: 401(k) info @ metlife.com.

EDUCATE-COMMUNICATE
Defined Contribution Group
✳ MetLife®

SCHULZ
PEANUTS © United Feature Syndicate, Inc.

96041A5R-MLIC-LD © 1996 Metropolitan Life Insurance Co., NY, NY

"We wanted to go with a company like that, not a bank or insurance company type of product," Martin says. "We wanted a public mutual fund company where you can look up your funds every day in *The New York Times*, *The Wall Street Journal* or the local paper and see how they're doing."

LOOKING AHEAD

Martin's primary concern for the future is how to grow his company. The 401(k) may help him to do just that. Although there have been no dramatic improvements directly attributable to the plan so far, he is pleased with how the incentive-based program is working and how well it has been accepted. "I sense a little bit more of a teamwork approach—employees all feel they're in the same boat," Martin says. "Another major accomplishment is that the plan has made us a more attractive employer. When we talk to new employees about our benefits package, they quickly see that with the 401(k), we are very competitive. I think we're having an easier time attracting new, qualified people than in the past."

Although the plan's administrative fees and match are expensive for the company, Martin thinks it's worth it. Those costs are more than offset by gains in productivity. His one complaint, however, is that certain members of management benefit less than the other employees, who may contribute from 1% to 15% of their salary. Members of top management are limited to a maximum of 4% to ensure that Bronson doesn't run afoul of non-discrimination regulations. "But in the end, helping the company is what helps me the most," Martin notes. "I think the program's been good for the company and will continue to be good for all of us over the long-term."

A 90% 401(k) participation rate reflects an impressive buy-in to Bronson's performance-based company match. Rewarding a company-wide commitment to quality and the achievement of shared goals appears to be a successful path toward a more secure financial future for the 70 employees of this small, private company.

MADISON AVENUE LURES THE 401(k) CONSUMER:
HOW A TURTLE BECAME THE BAIT

Coors Brewing Company
Golden, CO

Many companies would be satisfied with a 401(k) plan participation rate of 73% — but not Coors Brewing. In 1990 it set a higher goal and developed a masterpiece of marketing strategy that boosted participation to 89% in just ten months. Former benefits manager Rex Gooch applied advertising concepts to simple ideas having nothing to do with beer that were inexpensive to implement and are available to any plan sponsor.

> ➤ Brews and bottles beer
> ➤ 6,500 employees in 3 locations
> ➤ 89% participation rate
> ➤ 50 cents-on-the-dollar match to 6% of salary
> ➤ 401(k) plan assets: $350 million

The campaign to raise 401(k) plan participation grew out of a flow of employee feedback indicating that many older workers expected the company to take care of them for life. Learning that the Coors defined benefit pension plan might replace only 25% to 35% of their salary was a shock for many and a typical reaction was, "I wish I'd known about this ten or twenty years ago so I could have been saving." Roger Boman, Director of Compensation and Benefits, challenged the benefits team to increase 401(k) participation.

The company had a good 401(k) plan but had never promoted it. "We called the plan TERA, for Tax Effective Retirement Account, a name we ended up having to explain all the time. Some employees didn't even know it was a 401(k)," Gooch says.

A 401(k) MASCOT

The benefits staff decided the plan needed a mascot to create an appealing, easily recognizable identity. They mulled over ideas until Gooch came up with terrapin, the name for a type of freshwater turtle. A graphic artist drew a happy turtle standing on its hind legs, wearing running shoes and jogging down a path. This was early in 1990—before more famous cartoon turtles came on the scene.

Of course, a terrapin mascot required a TERA pin, so thousands of green and yellow enameled TERA Turtle lapel pins were ordered. Then table-tents were

STATE OF THE 401(k)

NYL Benefit Services Company, Inc.
A New York Life Company

TECHNOLOGIES

CLIENT SERVICES

401(K) COMPLETE

INVESTMENTS

COMMUNICATIONS

 To launch your plan into the 21st century, check out our web site (www.nylbsc.com), or call us at 1.800.586.1413 and we'll bring our interactive presentation to you.

placed on all the tables in the cafeteria; each had a sketch of the turtle and the words, "Coming Soon"—nothing else. A few weeks later, the turtle appeared on the front page of the company newspaper in an article that explained the 401(k) plan and introduced a promotional "drawing" created by the benefits department to attract attention and boost participation.

Lapel pins were sent to all plan participants and each name was put into a pot. Every week for six months a name was drawn and $100 in cash was awarded to the winning employee, provided that person was wearing a TERA Turtle pin on the day of the drawing. Non-participants received a letter extolling the benefits of the plan and explaining they could enter the drawing simply by returning an enclosed postcard requesting a projection of what their 401(k) savings would be at various rates of participation if they joined. The letter also enclosed an enrollment form. Employees did not have to join in order to win, but many people did as a result of the excitement generated by the promotion.

A tremendous groundswell of attention and conversation flooded the company. "Every time you went into the cafeteria, that's all people were talking about. In just a matter of two or three weeks, you couldn't find an employee who wasn't wearing the TERA pin," Gooch remembers.

Other promotional gimmicks followed: non-participants who joined the plan and participants who increased their contributions or were already contributing the maximum amount got a TERA Turtle coffee mug etched with the turtle jogging along a path toward a bush on the other side of the mug. As hot liquid was poured into the mug, the bush turned into a pot of gold with TERA written across it.

At the end of the six months, participation was up by 12%. Boman was so pleased he authorized the benefits department to keep the drawing going for another four months. When the promotion finally ended, participation increased by 16.5% to 89% and Coors had given away only $4,100. The success of that promotion also enabled the company to increase the contribution limit for highly compensated employees by 6%—from 9% to 15% of base pay—and continue to meet IRS non-discrimination requirements. The maximum contribution for non-highly compensated employees was, and remains, 17%.

Although the pins and mugs are no longer distributed, the mascot continues to enjoy its starring role on every piece of 401(k) literature. To this day, Coors reports, when employees see the TERA Turtle heading an article in the company newspaper, they tend to read it first because they know it's about their money, their savings.

THE FIXED-INCOME FIX

That original campaign included literature describing the plan's particular features. At the time, there were only two investment options: a GIC fund and an equity fund. 90% of participants put every penny into the fixed-income fund, partly because Coors had never provided any investment education, but also because the equity fund was not listed in newspapers and employees just didn't know much about it.

In 1992, the equity fund was replaced with a big name growth fund and three new options were added: a growth and income fund, an index fund and the Coors stock fund. The new investment options were introduced through home mailings featuring a colorful, easy-to-understand brochure that described the 401(k) plan basics and included a glossary on the last two pages explaining words like "index fund", "maturity" and "principal." Another fold-out brochure defined what a mutual fund is and used automobile speedometers to illustrate the risks and rewards of the various investment options.

"This was our first stab at talking about risk, and most of it dealt with general risk," says Gooch. "Since mutual funds were a new concept for most people, we were trying to get the point across that you have to take a little risk to get a better rate of return, but you have to expect some short-term fluctuation."

There were also presentations in the Coors auditorium to explain the plan and the new investments. Although the majority of Coors employees work at the main brewery in Golden, several hundred others are at two smaller sites in Tennessee and Virginia. Coors made a video for them. The lead-in highlighted Chairman Bill Coors talking about the importance of saving for your future. He explained that the company had made some great changes to the TERA program and told employees he was excited by the opportunities offered by the new mutual fund options. Then the video introduced the new funds with a segment on each, talked about diversification and repeated information employees missed if they couldn't attend the presentations.

While all this was going on, the benefits team was winning a battle to eliminate the restrictions that had plagued the old 401(k), such as limiting to four times a year participants' chances to change contribution amounts or move assets from one fund to another. "We had all these rules and the thought behind them was to keep the administration costs down," Gooch says. "My philosophy was to make it easier for employees to join the plan by eliminating a bunch of unnecessary, cumbersome restrictions that people used as excuses for not joining."

Although colleagues warned that eliminating them would force costs up, Gooch thought not. He argued that there would be increased activity for a few months while people played with the new freedoms, then activity would subside. And that's what happened. "People don't move their money around," he says. "Coors is pretty successful at communicating the message that this is long-term retirement money. Put it in there and leave it alone."

Two years later, the company introduced four new fund options: three asset manager funds and an overseas fund. The accompanying educational program included a personal profile questionnaire with twelve questions about risk and time left until retirement. The employee's answers suggested a category of assets appropriate for that profile. Coors credits the cumulative impact of all these efforts with lowering the plan's fixed-income investments from 90% of the total in 1992 to about 45% in 1996, and says the percentage continues to drop.

About a year after those asset manager funds were introduced, Coors surveyed a pre-selected group of participants whose investment choices were both diversified and not diversified. "70% of those people said, add more funds. We thought the non-diversified people would say we've got too many," Gooch notes. "Instead, we discovered that they really wanted to have new funds available when they diversified later on."

In 1996 Coors will introduce four more funds: blue chip, small-cap, equity income and another growth and income fund. The company plans another series of educational meetings to discuss investing; these meetings, however, will divide employees into target audiences and will be preceded by targeted mailings.

DIVIDE AND CONQUER

"You've got people enrolled in the 401(k) who are going in many different directions. They're in the plan for one reason, or not in it for another. Once they're in they're either too conservative or not very knowledgeable," Gooch explains. "If you try to make your message generic and reach everybody in one shot, it gets too complicated. There's too much competing information. Break it down into small bites of information. I think that's the key."

The letter that targeted non-participants a few years ago was so successful—it produced an 11.5% enrollment among non-participants—Coors decided more is better. This time, it divided the participant audience into four groups: the non-participants; those who are contributing less than 6%; those who are invested only in the fixed-income fund and those who are well diversified.

The letter to non-participants, for example, is very simple and similar to the one that worked so well before. It tells employees they're missing out on a pot of gold, illustrated at the end of a rainbow. It is personalized for each employee and explains how much a given contribution, plus company match, would amount to over different time periods.

For those participants who contributed less than 6% of their salary, Coors plans to use a chart describing how much company money they gave up. "The first column says this is what you're putting in—let's say, 2%. The next column says 4% and the next 6%, and under each it shows the amount of the company's matching contribution that person is missing out on. Then it shows how much that account would grow in five, ten, fifteen years," Gooch explains.

The letter to those fully invested in fixed-income uses pie charts. The first chart will be a fixed-income pie showing the average annual rate of return for the fixed-income fund in the three years since the equity mutual funds were introduced in June 1992. The second pie will show two funds: one-half growth, one-half fixed-income, with the corresponding average return for that mix. The third pie will show three funds: one-third growth, one-third growth and income and one-third fixed-income.

The message for participants who have diversified investments is: congratulations, *but*—although you are doing really well with your savings and investing, if you don't have a financial plan in place, you probably need one just to see if you're on track to meet your retirement goals. Then Coors lists different tools participants can use, including software programs and financial planning programs.

TARGETING MEETINGS FOR SPECIAL AUDIENCES

A series of employee meetings was organized, each built around a slightly different target audience. Two groups, non-participants and those saving less than 6%, were combined for very general, basic investment meetings that explained why they should be saving at least 6% of their wages.

Other meetings targeted non-diversified investors, and those for sophisticated investors covered advanced investment concepts, such as different investing styles

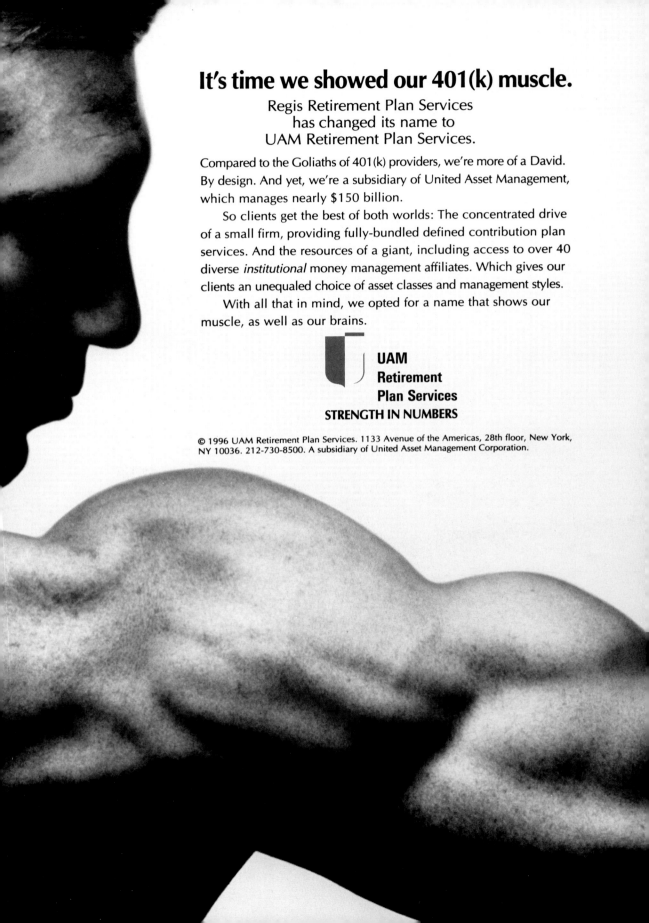

It's time we showed our 401(k) muscle.

Regis Retirement Plan Services has changed its name to UAM Retirement Plan Services.

Compared to the Goliaths of 401(k) providers, we're more of a David. By design. And yet, we're a subsidiary of United Asset Management, which manages nearly $150 billion.

So clients get the best of both worlds: The concentrated drive of a small firm, providing fully-bundled defined contribution plan services. And the resources of a giant, including access to over 40 diverse *institutional* money management affiliates. Which gives our clients an unequaled choice of asset classes and management styles.

With all that in mind, we opted for a name that shows our muscle, as well as our brains.

**UAM
Retirement
Plan Services**
STRENGTH IN NUMBERS

and investment fund managers' strategies. Coors also plans a meeting just for retirees to discuss their particular investment concerns and questions.

The meetings were advertised principally through postcards sent to everyone's home, listing all the meetings and their times and indicating which were appropriate for the recipient. Employees were told you can go to any meeting, but if you're a non-participant you should go to this one, if you're a non-diversified investor, go to that one.

Coors also found an innovative way to avoid postage costs for an effective elementary investment guide it wanted to distribute to employees. It is a slender volume but hard-backed, which made postage costs prohibitive. The benefits staff came up with the idea for a coupon that could be mailed with the letters. The coupon looks like a dollar bill, but the TERA Turtle replaces George Washington and the back side has instructions to take the coupon to the benefits department or to one of the employee meetings for a free gift: the investment book.

"Anytime you have a give-away like that, especially if there's some mystery to it, people want to participate," Gooch observes. "Coors will still have some mailing costs for people who are not nearby but it won't be much. We'll tell them to mail in their coupons and we'll send back the book."

LOOKING AHEAD

To appeal to more sophisticated investors and give them access to a wider universe of fund options, Coors is looking seriously at a self-directed brokerage account option which, at a small fee to participants, will allow them to move their money into any mutual fund. This recommendation went to the company's retirement committee in the Fall of 1996 for their review and approval.

The success Coors enjoys at boosting participation and increasing investment diversification rests heavily on its ability to generate employee interest and enthusiasm by sustaining a high level of employee comfort with the 401(k) plan. The company has used simple, inexpensive tools that borrow heavily on obvious Madison Avenue techniques to help employees connect in a continuing personal and meaningful way with *their* TERA Turtle and everything it represents.

CHAPTER SIX

A PROFIT-BASED MATCH:
MAKING EMPLOYEES FEEL LIKE SHAREHOLDERS

Kendall Packaging Corp.
Milwaukee, WI

Kendall Packaging started its 401(k) in late 1990 with a turbulent history and problems it hoped the plan would help resolve. After instituting a number of improvements, extensive employee communications and a remarkable policy of financial disclosure, the 401(k) plan did, indeed, meet Kendall's expectations.

> ➤ Designs and prints packaging (primarily for the food industry)
> ➤ 80 employees in 3 locations
> ➤ 92% 401(k) plan participation
> ➤ Profit-based company match adjusted quarterly
> ➤ 401(k) plan assets: $500 Million

Not only is Kendall's 401(k) company match based on company profits, this privately owned business reveals its profits, losses and future prospects to its employees every quarter with a candor rarely encountered anywhere else. In fact, it treats its employees much like shareholders.

That was not always the case. Kendall was once a union shop but, following a strike that began in 1988, replacement workers were hired, some old workers returned, the main plant moved out of Milwaukee to a suburban location, some new employees were hired, an employee vote led to decertification of the union and a subsequent organizing attempt was defeated. The result was tension between labor and management, which management acknowledged and wanted to resolve. Unsure of which issues to confront, Kendall took a company-wide survey.

A consulting firm was hired to develop the survey and ask questions about morale and attitude. James Baudhuin, vice president of finance, says the results showed that employees felt there was a lack of communication between labor and management, little management attention to employee needs and no follow-up on employees' suggestions or complaints. Baudhuin thought quarterly company-wide meetings would help address those concerns.

"I had been exposed to meetings like that at other companies in the past, so I felt very comfortable giving employees information on how the company was doing," he says. "I had always felt that employees—given information on company profits and performance—would take a more active role and really feel they were contributing. We had been promoting the team concept but it was as though we were asking employees to play on our team without giving them the game score."

Kendall's president and chairman, Eric Erickson, was committed to the team concept and wanted employees to participate in company profits but, initially, it was difficult for him to go so far as to disclose profits and other financial data. Ultimately, however, he agreed that quarterly meetings and financial disclosure were the best ways to solve problems identified by the survey and implement a realistic profit-sharing program.

PHASING OUT DB...SWITCHING TO DC

When the company announced in 1990 that it was setting up a 401(k) plan, it simultaneously announced that it would terminate the old pension plan which, Baudhuin says, had become an expensive nuisance. All the required government regulations made it too complicated and costly for such a small company and he felt a DB plan wasn't much of an incentive for young employees who usually place little value on a benefit they would receive 30 years in the future. Kendall froze its DB plan for five years while it resolved an underfunding problem—the real nuisance—and made the preparations necessary to terminate the program.

The 401(k), set up to take over retirement benefits from the DB plan, started with a small 12$^{1}/_{2}$ cents-on-the-dollar company match, up to 6% of salary, which was quickly raised to 25 cents. The idea of turning the company match into a profit-sharing program evolved. "We liked the idea of tying profit-sharing to the 401(k) as an inducement for the employees to participate in their own retirement planning—and it worked," Baudhuin says.

In its first couple of years, the 401(k) plan attracted a 65% to 70% participation rate, Baudhuin recalls, then jumped to over 80% when profit-sharing started in 1993. It jumped again to about 92% when a new investment program with improved communications was initiated this year.

The match currently fluctuates with profits, to as high as 70% of the first 6% of wages. "But we can see it reaching 150% or 200% of the first 6%," Baudhuin says. "Maybe we'll move it up to 9% of salary to encourage higher contributions from our employees."

The match was 50% for the first half of this year. It is calculated by Baudhuin after he looks at the company's performance for the quarter and makes a recommendation to the chairman. They know what a 100% match would be and they add or subtract from that based on their profit level. At the end of the first quarter of 1996, Baudhuin recommended cutting the match to zero for the next quarter because the company only broke even. The chairman rejected that proposal, saying they had record orders in December and January, were working on record orders for February and had been named Supplier of The Year by two major accounts. Based on business forecasts, he felt the employees deserved a reward; the match remained at 50%.

COMMUNICATING WITH THE TROOPS

Baudhuin describes Kendall's employee communications and education program as an ongoing commitment. It includes a newsletter published in the first month of each quarter, 401(k) statements and employee meetings in the second month, investment or contribution changes in the third month plus bulletin board post-ings and the distribution of other information as needed. A 24-hour 800-number was recently added.

There are six employee meetings each quarter: one at headquarters, two at the Jefferson, Wisconsin plant and three at the company's other plant in Pittsburgh, Kansas. Multiple meetings mean production does not stop: employees either stay an hour late or come in an hour early, and Baudhuin says they do attend. He esti-mates that it took a year or so of quarterly meetings until the employees began to digest all the information they were getting and feel comfortable with the format.

"We toss a P&L up on an overhead screen and talk a little bit about compar-isons to last year, how we're doing this quarter versus the same quarter last year, year-to-date versus the same period last year and how the other plant is doing," Baudhuin explains. "They're team members, but they're also a little competitive. We show a consolidated income statement and everyone sees how the company as a whole did for the quarter."

He also shows a chart that explains how 401(k) plan assets have grown, makes a pitch for participating and for increasing contribution levels to the maximum and answers any questions. Now, he says, everyone is interested in incoming orders, shipments and backlogs because they see how directly every component of the business affects profits and their own company match. "People in the shop come up with ideas for saving waste. People in the shop complain about scrap. There's an awareness of what impacts their profit-sharing contribution. At the last meeting one employee asked me if I fly first class or coach."

Baudhuin believes the meetings have opened up a dialogue between workers and management so that employees now feel free to raise a problem or question with an executive who is walking through the plant. He is convinced, as well, that the meetings have improved morale and performance. "They created a pressure-release valve. The employees know there's a quarterly meeting coming up, so if they really have a beef, they can bring it up at the meeting," he explains.

The company experimented briefly with a gain-sharing program. "We print on fairly expensive film, so scrap is very important," Baudhuin explains. "Productivity is important, but since we are material intensive, shaving minutes or pennies off labor costs doesn't amount to a great deal. Our business is volume-sensitive and it's hard for our employees to make a significant impact on the problem other than by controlling material costs and indirect labor." That proved to be one more argument for profit-sharing.

SPELLING OUT THE DETAILS

The company newsletter, like the meetings, developed as a response to the results of the employee survey. It was something the company had always talked about doing but had never quite gotten around to until the marketing director finally took it on. But he had designed it as a marketing tool directed to clients and potential customers even though it was also distributed to employees. Baudhuin and a marketing department assistant developed an alternative: an in-house newsletter that featured news of the 401(k) program, listed winners of softball and bowling contests and included notes on other local, company-related events.

One of Baudhuin's most innovative ideas was to use the company bulletin boards to discuss news events affecting the 401(k) plan. For example, when a story broke about the Labor Department investigation of companies that did not deposit their employee contributions promptly into participant 401(k) accounts, Baudhuin immediately put up a notice explaining Kendall policy and procedures. He detailed the process his office uses to deposit the funds, assured everyone that the plan undergoes an annual audit and invited anyone with questions to call him directly.

WATCH THOSE INTEREST-FREE LOANS TO UNCLE SAM

When he heard an employee bragging about a big tax refund, Baudhuin hastened to compose a notice for the bulletin boards that started, "Getting a nice refund from the IRS this year? Isn't that just great…you've been making an interest-free loan to Uncle Sam all year…" It goes on to say what an employee should do instead—put a little more into the 401(k) every month. With the profit-sharing match, that extra contribution would have turned that particular employee's $360 refund into $635.

Every quarter he posts the 401(k) plan's mutual fund results for the preceding quarter and the year-to-date. Since its inception, Kendall's 401(k) plan offered one stock fund, one bond fund and one money market fund, with recordkeeping managed by another vendor. But the mutual funds experienced a couple of years of below-par performance and Baudhuin started to look for some alternatives. "At first, there was so little money in the plan that a point or two in performance didn't matter much. But when we terminated our DB plan last year, employees rolled their DB assets into their 401(k)s and some people were building up pretty serious amounts in their retirement accounts. When those numbers get up to $30,000, $40,000 we have to pay more attention," he says.

After a review and analysis of other options, Kendall selected a local mutual fund company with solid performance, excellent reputation and a comprehensive service package. It offered a 24-hour 800-number to process enrollment and investment changes without paper forms and agreed to visit all the Kendall plants and meet with employees at no extra cost.

At the next quarterly employee meeting, Baudhuin steered the discussion in the direction he wanted it to go—investment options and better communications, and asked what improvements employees would like to see. "Well, comments started popping up. 'I'd like to see an international fund, I'd like to see a small-cap fund.' I tell you, our employees are sitting in the lunchroom reading *Money* magazine!" Baudhuin exclaims. "Particularly our Kansas group. It tends to be a little older, tighter-knit group and when our employees get together, they compare investment information."

The next newsletter reviewed the discussions at the employee meetings and explained how the company was working on responding to employee requests. The following month, a three-page letter went out to all employees announcing the selection of the new investment company, explaining all the details of the conversion and the features of the new program. It also listed the dates of the next company employee meetings. The letters were accompanied by a packet of information prepared by the fund company that included profiles of each of the new funds as well as enrollment forms.

Instead of the three investment options previously available, the new selection

The PRISM 401(k) plan from Key is designed to help employees manage their 401(k) themselves. Our comprehensive array of educational materials and a 24-hour 800 number for balance and investment transfers put more control in their hands— and more time on yours. And PRISM offers a wide selection of fund options with a record of strong performance. To learn more about the benefits of PRISM, call 1-800-303-9826.

PRISM® 401(k) PLAN

More control for employees.
Less work for you.

Sounds like a plan.

Key. For a new America.^{SM}

offers eight: money market, government securities, corporate bonds, balanced, international equity, capital appreciation and two growth funds. The fund company provides a monthly report listing each fund's performance—which Baudhuin can post on the bulletin boards without having to prepare his own. "The employees feel management listened and everyone was delighted with the first presentation the fund company put on for us," Baudhuin says.

He is now occupied by the transition from the old fund company to the new one and the job of educating everyone about the new investment options and services available. Baudhuin's regular communications program will continue as usual; the new presentations and information will merely be additions.

After these changes have been absorbed and everything has returned to normal, Kendall may decide to do another employee survey. "I'd like to update it, see if we've addressed all the problems, find out if there are any new ones," he says. "I want to see if the things we've done over the last three years have improved the morale of the organization. I think they have."

CHAPTER SEVEN

FRIENDLY, FUNNY AND FAMILIAR:
401(k) COMMUNICATIONS THAT WORK

J.P. Morgan & Co., Inc.
New York, NY

E ven a world-famous banking institution like J.P. Morgan, with a corporate culture preoc- cupied with maximizing shareholder value, can't presume that every one of its employees will under- stand how the company's 401(k) plan works—or appreciate the necessity to save for their retirement.

Morgan's defined contribution plan, in place since 1959, allowed employees to decide how much of their annual profit-sharing award they wanted paid in cash and how much they would set aside in a tax-deferred retirement account. Contributions to the deferred accounts were invested in the firm's own institutional commingled funds by Morgan's asset management unit. A variety of recent tax reforms, however, led Morgan to drop that annual selection and mandate a simple half and half split: 50% paid in cash and 50% deferred. In response to complaints from employees who wanted to defer more than 50%, Morgan established a 401(k) plan in 1993 but, with both a defined benefit pension plan and a rich profit-sharing plan that has averaged 15%, Morgan does not offer its employees the lure of a 401(k) with a matching company contribution.

Despite its in-house focus on money and investing, Morgan has as much trouble as any other company getting people to join the 401(k) plan, according to Gary Naylor, Profit-Sharing/401(k) Plan Administrator. "Today's typical new employee focuses on his or her career; signing up for benefit programs gets pushed to the back of their minds. Although the investment challenge here—to provide enough options—may differ because our employees have a real appetite for that, I don't think our problems getting people to participate are any different."

When Morgan decided to launch its 401(k), Naylor expected senior people to part- icipate to the maximum allowed, but he knew that lower compensated employees

> Global investment bank and securities firm

> 10,000 U.S. employees eligible for 401(k) plan

> 70% participation, no company match

> Defined benefit and profit-sharing plan

> 401(k) plan assets exceed $800 million

needed something special to attract their attention and get them on board. The solution included a video that entertains and educates employees as it introduces and explains both the 401(k) plan and Morgan's new group of investment options.

SEEING IS BELIEVING

The video—original, friendly, funny and useful—could be a model for any plan sponsor. Although Morgan outsourced its production, Naylor and his team collaborated closely in designing the film, writing the script and selecting the narrator, a man in his 50s or 60s with a Walter Cronkite image. "That was exactly what we wanted to project," explains Naylor. "This is not rocket science and you can trust this individual." They were also careful to keep the visuals personal and local, featuring lots of employee interviews and familiar street scenes from the Wall Street neighborhood where most Morgan employees work.

Morgan built the 20-minute video around a series of "commercials" that introduce or comment on segments in which the narrator discusses different aspects and benefits of saving through the 401(k). This innovative structure allows Morgan to change any segment as it becomes outdated, or alter the voice-over and leave the visual alone to suit specific needs without having to redo the whole video.

It also gave Morgan the flexibility to use the video to promote the 401(k) plan without having to show all 20 minutes: they spliced just the funny, commercial-style vignettes into a video loop that ran continuously for a month prior to the beginning of the 401(k) program. Monitors were set up in heavily trafficked locations—the entrance to the lunchroom, among others—and the video invited everyone to attend a seminar and learn more about how participating in the 401(k) plan can help them plan and save for a secure retirement.

"We tried to make it humorous," Naylor says. "People need entertainment." And entertaining it is. The video opens with a 30-second introduction: a small, cheap car is driven around a curve while the narrator intones, "This little piggy never saved for retirement." A full-size sedan follows as the narrator says, "This little piggy saved but put his money in the wrong place." Finally, a chauffeured limousine speeds around the same curve while the narrator concludes, smugly, "This little piggy used a 401(k). Now he's being driven all the way home. 401(k)—you're never too old for a piggy bank."

The video continues with a segment that lasts a minute and a half: the narrator discusses the benefits of saving in general, and in pre-tax dollars in particular. It cuts to "Word on the Street," 60 seconds of various Morgan employees talking about why saving is important to them and how even a little bit of saving is better than no saving at all. The title of the segment is a play on the name of *The Wall Street Journal* column "Heard on the Street" and on broadcasting's "Man On the Street."

The video goes on at its lively pace with additional "Word on the Street" segments followed by narration on the tax benefits of 401(k)s, how easy it is to save when deductions are taken out of your paycheck and how quickly a participant's money can grow. One "Word on the Street" segment includes clips of people out on the street who respond to the question, "What is a 401(k)?" Answers include "a Mercedes Benz" and "a breakfast cereal".

Another segment follows a young man through his typical day, adding up all the things he spends money on, from buying a shirt to paying for dinner and a movie with his girlfriend, while he complains bitterly about how he can't afford to save. The day's expenses: more than $200. The narrator has a few things to say about that, as well.

GETTING SMARTER AT LUNCH

The 1993 video series did its job; thousands of people showed up at the investment seminars. "They were all voluntary, lunchtime seminars," Naylor says, and on average, each seminar drew 100 to 200 people. Participants at each of the 30 seminars saw the entire video after a presentation about the 401(k) plan features and before an investment manager described the variety of investment options. A slide presentation highlighting key points from the video followed; then the floor opened for questions and answers.

Naylor believes these meetings are most effective if he uses different presentation methods (video, slides, presenters) to vary the pace and the delivery; that also allows enough repetition to make sure the important points get across. He follows the same format every time the seminar is offered. New employees and anyone else who wants to attend are welcome.

Although most of Morgan's U.S. employees work at its Wall Street offices, approximately 1,300 systems and operations people are at a site in Delaware. The same seminar travels there twice each year. Other, smaller offices get copies of the video. Since its inception, the video has been updated three times and several segments have been used in other company-wide presentations.

DEADBEAT LETTERS: A POWERFUL TOOL

As a result of those initial presentations, more than 50% of Morgan's employees signed up for the 401(k) in 1993. Participation is now up to 70%, and 300 to 400 employees are pulled into the plan each year by Naylor's now infamous April 15th personalized "deadbeat letters," a powerful tool for increasing participation and riveting individual investment self-awareness.

While many benefit managers send out letters pointing out how much money non-participants give up by failing to join the company 401(k) plan, Morgan sends out annual tax-time letters pointing out how big a tax deduction they are handing back to Uncle Sam. Naylor is in cahoots with the payroll department, which figures out the deduction for each of the nearly 2,000 employees who receive a personal letter every year.

Last year's letter said, "In a world of constant change, there's one thing you can count on. I'm still here... I'm not going to rest until you join the Morgan 401(k). You know you need to save money for your future and I'm sure you wouldn't mind cutting your taxes now..." And for a particular employee it continued, "If you had saved just 3% through the Morgan 401(k) last year, you would have reduced your 1994 taxable income by $1,278." Then it pointed out that 3% of this employee's salary would only take $38.25 out of her paycheck in after-tax dollars, an amount equal to $53.25 of pre-tax dollars invested.

This year's letter says, "If you had saved just 3% of your income last year, you would have reduced your taxable income by $xxx. And if that doesn't make you feel bad, how about this: Last year was one of the best years ever for stocks and bonds and you missed it. All 10 funds in the 401(k) posted solid gains. In fact, the Equity Fund was up 38.7%! Did you do that well on your own?"

The letters work. Not only do they attract hundreds of new participants each year, other employees actually call to apologize for not joining. "I find it very interesting to hear feedback from people who try to explain to me why they don't participate," Naylor says. "When someone has what they think is a legitimate reason not to participate, I explain that I am very pleased they have thought it out. I don't have a problem with that."

OTHER TOOLS

Although almost 80% to 90% of Morgan's employees have computers, the company uses a telephone voice response system for enrollment, switching investments, arranging loans and checking on personal account balances. Morgan decided on an 800-number system so that anyone could access the system anytime from anywhere. The program currently offers monthly valuations, but Morgan is considering switching to daily valuation.

An outside vendor supplies quarterly newsletters on financial planning and Morgan itself produces an assortment of printed materials on the profit sharing/ 401(k) plan. Each participant receives a personal, quarterly account statement with a pie chart on its cover that illustrates how that person's money is invested by fund type, (i.e., equity, diversified, international, fixed-income, etc.). Inside the four-page statement is a breakdown of the account by fund, earnings, deposits, withdrawals and fund transfers. On its back is a performance chart listing all ten Morgan investment options and the indexes against which they may be judged, such as the S&P 500, the Consumer Price Index and the Ibbotson Sinquefield Treasury Bill Index.

Every Thanksgiving, Morgan sends out an "annual report" that explains the 401(k) plan in detail, emphasizing the benefits of diversification and describing each of the available investment options with a pie chart to show each fund's holdings. The annual report also includes a total return performance chart with 3, 5, 10 and 15-year numbers and a growth chart that shows how a $10,000 investment in each fund fared over 10 years compared to relevant indexes.

MEASURING SUCCESS

As participation levels increase, diversification is less of a problem than it was a few years ago. In 1988, 19% of plan assets were in company stock, 5% were in U.S. equities, 66% were in fixed-income and 10% were in balanced funds. By 1996, those numbers had shifted significantly to 16% in company stock, 23% in U.S. equities, 25% in fixed-income, 19% in a balanced fund and 17% in international equities. In addition to company stock, Morgan's investment choices now include emerging markets, U.S. small companies, international equities, U.S. large-cap equities, diversified U.S. stocks and bonds, U.S. corporate and government bonds,

insured contracts, money market and a global strategies mix of equity, fixed-income and real estate.

Attributing the shift in diversification in part to Morgan's particular company-wide "culture," as well as to the investor education program, Naylor notes that "When I started at Morgan, people were much older and had much longer service with the company than they typically do now. The average age now is probably closer to the early 30s and the average length of service may be only six or seven years, so investments more appropriately match their age and the number of years they have till retirement."

LIFESTYLE FUNDS: A POTENTIAL DANGER

One fund type Morgan does not offer is the so-called lifestyle fund that creates a mix of investments for those who identify themselves as conservative, moderate or aggressive investors. Naylor thinks those funds are dangerous.

"As the years go on, if investors don't get their 10% return or whatever, I wonder if they'll come back to the plan sponsors and say, 'Well, you picked the profile, you picked the mix, but I only got 8% and it's your fault.' The purpose of a defined contribution plan was to give people flexibility, but the individual was taking on the investment risk. I'm not sure that it will always be viewed that way if the plan sponsor created the mix for that person."

He is also concerned about employees borrowing heavily against their 401(k) and then separating from employment. "The loans become due at that point, so not only does the employee have a tax burden on his hands because the loan is treated as a withdrawal if he doesn't have the funds to pay it off, but he's also lost some of his account value," he says.

THE BOTTOM LINE

Morgan's efforts to educate its employees about the benefits of participating in the company 401(k) plan continue to be a success story. Participation increases annually and Morgan has managed to convert more and more participants from savers into long-term, informed investors: growing diversification suggests that participants are shifting into investment options that carry higher levels of acceptable risk; their investment behavior is changing to meet their real retirement needs.

What makes the Morgan program so successful? Naylor understands his audience and responds to their needs and the ways they learn best by building a program that uses a variety of educational tools to reinforce one another, repeat important messages and reward a participant with specific, personalized information. Morgan understands the importance of a long-term, continuing commitment to 401(k) education. The results prove that their investment in it is paying off.

CHAPTER EIGHT

SPEAKING THE EMPLOYEE LANGUAGE:
TURNING MULTI-CULTURAL SPENDERS INTO SAVERS

Sterile Concepts, Inc.
Richmond, VA

A participation rate of 60% does not sound like much until you realize that Sterile Concepts employs a largely unskilled workforce whose average wage is about $17,000 a year, where Cambodian, Vietnamese or Spanish is the principal language of more than a third of the workers and just 12% are salaried employees. Moreover, the plan became effective only in January 1996—all of which makes 60% sound like a remarkable feat.

> ➤ Produces custom procedure trays for healthcare industry
> ➤ 1,000 employees in 3 locations
> ➤ 60% participation in 401(k)
> ➤ 50 cents-on-the-dollar match
> ➤ 401(k) plan assets: $1.4 million

Sterile Concepts went public in October 1994 in a spin-off from its parent, Carilion Health Systems, a non-profit hospital management company that offered its employees a pension plan but no defined contribution plan. Elissa Ecker, Director of Human Resources for Sterile Concepts, says its management and sales personnel always wanted a 401(k) but were concerned that employees whose starting wage is only $5.02 an hour would find it difficult to save.

"We felt we had a responsibility to maintain the defined benefit plan for the employees who had had it all along, so in our minds it wasn't feasible to simply switch to a 401(k)," Ecker explains. Sterile Concepts carved its employees' share of the money out of Carilion's DB plan and made that the base of its own defined benefit plan. The problem then was how to add a 401(k) and attract sufficient participation to make it viable.

"Our employees had trouble understanding our defined benefit plan, so how in the world could we get them to understand a 401(k) plan?" Ecker asks. "They weren't savers because many were living from paycheck to paycheck."

Ecker tackled the challenge with a logical first step: she sent out bids and selected a benefits consultant who organized focus groups to see if a 401(k) made sense. Would employees with low incomes be willing to put aside even 1% of their pay? To Ecker's surprise, the answer was a resounding yes.

TURNING SPENDERS INTO SAVERS

The plan Ecker and her associates developed is fairly standard: it offers a 50 cents-on-the-dollar match for up to 6% of pay to anyone with one year of service; the plan fully vests after five years. Employees who had been with the company before the IPO were given credit for their years of service, so many were vested immediately. Minimum employee contributions are just 1%; the maximum is 12%. Ecker and the benefits consultant took this plan outline back to the focus groups and, with their blessing, started designing a communications and education program to sell it.

Coincidentally, while these initial steps were being taken, Sterile Concepts acquired two smaller companies in the same business—one in Minnesota with 80 employees and one in California with 250. Each company already had a 401(k) but no pension plan, so the 401(k)s had to be consolidated and their workers introduced to the Sterile Concepts program. Ecker capitalized on a strong selling point: everyone was gaining retirement money they hadn't had before. Sterile Concepts had a DB plan and was going to get a 401(k); the two acquired companies had 401(k)s and would gain a pension plan. The education program would explain both sides of the benefits.

In Ecker's continuing view, the world is made up of spenders, savers and investors. "The majority of our employees are probably spenders and we need to transform them into savers. Very few are investors—whether they're hourly workers or salaried employees. In fact, communication with our workforce was just as difficult with those who spoke English. Very few understood fixed-income or bonds versus stocks. Whether English was their first language or not, there was a problem."

The crux of the education program was a series of employee meetings on company time offered in four languages: Vietnamese, Cambodian and English in Richmond; Spanish and English at the California plant; English alone in Minnesota. There was no shortage of meetings: 35 in Richmond, seven in California and another three in Minnesota were held so each could accommodate a small group of 25 to 30 employees and everyone could sign up for the language of their choice at a convenient time.

Once the meeting schedule was set, Ecker began distributing flyers to attract attention. All were short, funny and written in very simple English.

One showed a teacher standing at a blackboard that said:

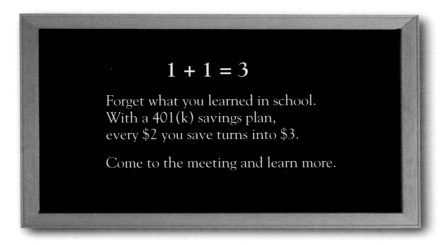

$$1 + 1 = 3$$

Forget what you learned in school.
With a 401(k) savings plan,
every $2 you save turns into $3.

Come to the meeting and learn more.

Another showed a dog chewing on the enrollment form and said: "What's your excuse for not signing up for the 401(k) savings plan?

a) I can't afford it.
b) I'll start next year.
c) I'm too young to think about retirement.
d) I put my money in the bank.
e) My dog ate my enrollment form.

No more excuses! The time to start saving is now. Learn more at your 401(k) meeting."

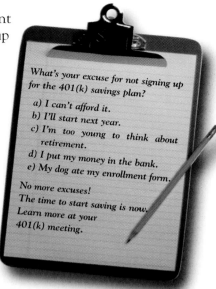

SELLING THE PLAN

Last and best was the flyer distributed to employees as they walked into each meeting. It said: "What's more than okay? The 401(k). Where else can you put $2 into a savings account and get $3?"

It pictured two $1 bills and had a silver dollar glued on top. Then it continued: "Don't miss out on one of the best ways you have to save."

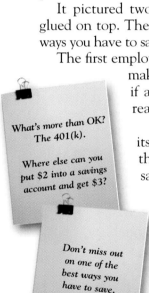

The first employee meeting was held for department heads and vice presidents to make sure they understood the program and could explain it to others if asked. Ecker wanted to make sure that there were more people ready to answer questions than just she and her three-person staff.

The meetings were conducted jointly by Sterile Concepts and its mutual fund provider, whose representatives began by explaining the new retirement program, 401(k) plan, company match, tax savings, vesting and investment choices.

Their explanation of the investment options also included some elementary discussion of risk and reward, how to keep pace with inflation, different risk levels for different ages, how to make time work for you and the need to reevaluate your investments throughout various phases of your life.

Discussions of the loan option were well received; its availability alleviated employee concerns about getting access to their money in an emergency. "But the loans are a minimum of $1,000 so we told people, if you need a new refrigerator and you only have $300 in the plan, you're not going to be able to get it out through the loan feature," Ecker explains. "We also stressed that this money is for *retirement* and they would only be able to take the money out for real hardship."

After their presentation on the plan basics, the mutual fund representatives projected onto a large overhead screen a customized computer program that was calibrated perfectly for the Sterile Concept audiences. "It was culturally diverse. Every ethnic group we have here was represented on screen. There were young people, single mothers and people nearing retirement, and it had humor," Ecker says. "It revolves around a retirement party. Faces appear and there are little asides about their dreams and aspirations. There's something in it everybody could relate to."

Each presentation was customized for its audience. Examples of people making $12,000 a year with calculations based on that amount were used for the production and warehouse audiences. For the sales representatives, the program used salaries and modeling projections based on a more relevant base salary. The presenters even used Ecker as an example to demonstrate how much more money she would have had at age 65 if she had started saving at 25 instead of at 35. The presenters took off their jackets and rolled up their sleeves for the hourly employees, but kept their jackets on and their ties tied for the sales and management group. Everyone was made to feel comfortable; the examples were realistic and hit home.

After the mutual fund representatives finished their presentations, Ecker or her assistant spoke, reiterating the main points of the program and emphasizing the importance of saving. "My parting words to every single group I addressed were, 'Don't be embarrassed to save just 1% of your salary. Take pride in the fact that you're saving for retirement.'"

"By the time the program ended, people realized that they couldn't live on just their defined benefit and Social Security payments, if in fact they will collect any Social Security," she continues. "The average age of our employees is 39, so is Social Security going to be there when they're ready to retire? I think the possibility that it might not be made an indelible impression."

The meetings held in Cambodian and Vietnamese were translated by employees who were also fluent in English. The Spanish-speaking meetings held at the California plant were run by a bilingual speaker who used a slide presentation prepared in Spanish rather than the computer program, but Ecker says the provider is preparing a Spanish-language version of the computer program.

Enrollment forms were distributed at each meeting and everyone was encouraged to take them home, read them and enroll. Many did so. "We went back to those who chose not to enroll," Ecker says. "That's what we have to do with most plans, regardless of what benefit it is. We have to go back to the employee again and help them fill out the forms."

SURPRISING ENROLLMENT RESULTS

Over 60% of the eligible enrollees had enrolled by the cut-off date—a terrific victory. Diversification rates were an even bigger surprise.

To keep things very simple, the plan initially offered just four investment choices: a fixed-income fund, a balanced fund, a growth and income stock fund and Sterile Concepts common stock. When Ecker tallied up the enrollments, she found that 51% went into the growth and income fund, 18% into the balanced fund, 16% into the income fund and 15% into company stock.

The Retirement Program Highlights brochure's risk/reward graph lists company stock as the riskiest investment and the growth and income fund next. "I was surprised," Ecker notes. "We were pleased to discover that our employees were willing to take a little more risk than we anticipated."

Ecker wants to add two or three funds this year, but has not decided which ones yet. She is also planning a new round of employee meetings for this summer that, in line with her commitment to move people along the curve from spending to saving to investing, will talk more about investing and investment options than

WHEN CHOOSING
A PROVIDER FOR YOUR 401(k), DEFINED BENEFIT,

OR YOUR

40 3 (b)

PROGRAM,

THERE ARE 2 WAYS TO GO:

WITH A PROVIDER THAT DOES A LITTLE OR A LOT

OF EVERYTHING OR

A PARTNER WHO DOES 1 THING AND DOES IT...

VERY WELL INDEED.

Today, we manage over $9 billion in retirement plan assets ~ providing investment and recordkeeping services and helping over 300,000 participants save and invest wisely for retirement. And that's all we do. To see what such single-minded attention might mean for your organization's retirement program, *call* Chris Cumming, Vice President, at 1-800-770-6797.

DIVERSIFIED INVESTMENT ADVISORS

Partners in Retirement Solutions

DIV95-1
REV. 8/96

last year's meeting's were able to do. Working with a benefits consultant, she plans to produce workbooks for participants, perhaps do a video and have her staff trained so they can do the complete presentations themselves.

"Our employees need visuals and they need to hear information," Ecker says. "With anything that's even a little bit complicated, you can't just hand employees reading material. They'll throw it into a corner of their desks or into the back of their lockers. You need to go out and make sure they can hear it, see it and understand it."

An 800-number to the mutual fund company will also be available as soon as the 401(k) plans of the two acquired companies are fully consolidated and reconciled with Sterile Concept's plan. That direct, fully accessible 24-hour line will allow employees to check their balances, switch investments daily and do some loan modeling. "If employees aren't comfortable using it, they can come to the HR department and we'll dial the number and walk through it together until they are comfortable," Ecker says. "We do stuff like that here." In fact, her department is open from 6:30 am to 5:00 pm every day to make sure the overnight shift, from 11:00 pm to 7:00 am, has access to her staff as well.

After a few quarterly statements go out showing how much the company match means to participants, Ecker thinks word of mouth will prod others to join. She expects that the 401(k) participation rate will eventually reflect the company's attention to employee concerns and its care in choosing communication tools that meet the real needs of their particular employee population. "We're also trying to create better communications for our defined benefit plan. We'll be sending out yearly statements on that, too. We've rarely done that in the past," Ecker says, as she anticipates future challenges and victories.

CHAPTER NINE

KEEP IT SIMPLE:
STRATEGIES THAT SPARK EMPLOYEE INTEREST INTO ACTION

TRINOVA Corp.
Maumee, OH

T RINOVA Corporation is a melting pot of many small companies acquired since 1916—each with its own retirement and medical plan—and thousands of employees spread out over more than 50 locations in the U.S. alone. Benefits implementation was understandably unwieldy and coordinated communications virtually impossible. In the late 1980s the company decided to consolidate individual benefit programs, simultaneously phasing out all its non-union defined benefit plans in favor of a single company-wide 401(k) plan plus profit-sharing.

> ➤ Manufactures fluid-, power- and motion-control equipment
> ➤ 16,000 employees worldwide
> ➤ 10,000 in U.S. in 50+ locations
> ➤ 73% 401(k) participation rate
> ➤ Profit-sharing plus 401(k)
> ➤ 75% match on first 4% of salary
> ➤ 401 (k) plan assets: $532 million

"Making these changes has been difficult, but from a philosophical viewpoint we are convinced that when employees have a stake in the company they are more productive and involved," says Patricia Krakos, the former Director of Benefits Planning and Administration. "The better the company does, the better they do." Although complicated, the process capitalized on educational and communications opportunities to raise participation 9% in two-and-a-half years and increase investment diversification even more.

Participation might be higher were it not for TRINOVA's generous profit-sharing plan, which gives every employee an annual 401(k) contribution of at least 1% of salary and sometimes considerably more, whether the employee contributes or not. One subsidiary's 1995 shared profit totaled 12% of salary. Putting that kind of money in an employee's 401(k) plan can make people feel they're well covered and do not need to contribute themselves. Combating that misconception is what pushed Krakos' efforts into high gear.

One theme she emphasized in company communications was how much money employees left on the table by failing to contribute at least 4% to their own 401(k) plan. The company matches dollar for dollar on the first 2% of salary

To know us is to know

and 50 cents-on-the-dollar for the next 2% for a total of 75% on the first 4% of salary, up to Federal maximums. New employees can join the 401(k) program after 90 days and the company match vests immediately. The profit-sharing, 25% of which goes into company stock, vests at 25% a year. Krakos calculated that employees forfeited $1.6 million in 1995 alone, and pointed out that by not contributing the full 4%, an employee gives up an immediate 75% rate of return.

SAVVY COMMUNICATIONS STYLE

"Prior to 1992, our communications efforts were probably typical of many manufacturing companies: lots of words, lots of information. We weighed the success of a communication piece by how long it was and how often we used words no one could understand," she laughs, remembering early efforts and adding that both employees and employer treated the new 401(k) with the same benign neglect they had given the old pension plan.

But benefits issues were becoming more complicated as laws and regulations changed and corporations were trying to evolve from paternal into "partner" organizations. It quickly became obvious that communicating the new issues in the old language didn't work, so Krakos sat down with her counterpart in the corporate communications department and asked, "How can we make this simpler? How can we make sure they get the message?"

The result uses *USA Today*-style color, graphics and bite-sized information in flyers that TRINOVA mails to everyone at home and distributes throughout the company, as well. The first flyer in 1992 was a general information piece on the 401(k) plan.

It featured a wide, gray margin on the left with the new script logo: *"What You Should Know About..."* A black-on-white headline announces: "TRINOVA's Retirement Savings Plan's 401(k)," and below it, on a bright blue background, a dime is divided into a pie showing where the $375 million in plan assets came from. Below that little icons show where the money was invested. For example, a TRINOVA star indicates the company stock fund, a piggy bank symbolizes the fixed-income fund. In the bottom right hand corner on a green background a body-shaped icon appears showing how many employees participate in the plan.

The back side of the flyer features a multicolor chart that describes briefly each investment option and its rate of return. Below it are three short news items illustrated with yellow-on-black headlines: one explains the difference between pre-tax and after-tax contributions using bites out of a dime on a purple background as a visual representation of the concept.

"This was a big step for us," Krakos notes. "It's a colorful, user-friendly change from the way we had done things in the past and the reaction was tremendous. Phones started ringing, employees started calling." Over the next six months employees in focus groups were asked what they thought of the flyer. They said they liked the style and the small bits of information presented in simple language that didn't need a lawyer's interpretation. And they liked having the flyers mailed

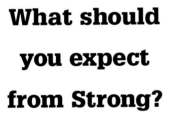

home, something the company did previously only for things like proxy materials.

"We find the most productive way by far to distribute information is to mail it home," Krakos explains. "It's more expensive, but in many cases the decision maker is not just our employee; it's often the spouse, as well. Even if it is just the employee, when you work in a plant environment you really have very little time during the day to look at something like that. Your time to read it, discuss it, is at home and we get a much better response using this approach."

There were a few negative comments in the focus groups about the cost of producing the four-color flyer and Krakos says people were amazed when they were told that they cost more to mail than to produce, thanks to the economies of computer graphics. The flyers have since become the principal vehicle for written communication. Occasionally, when issues need to be explained at greater length, a flyer will be produced in a four-page Q&A format. The flyers are not sent out too often to ensure that they remain special and employees don't lose interest in them. "Now we find that if we go for very long without producing one of these, people start asking when they'll be getting another one."

CHANGE EQUALS EDUCATIONAL OPPORTUNITY

One three-page self-mailer in 1994 announced changes in the 401(k) plan, introduced a new selection of funds and notified employees of upcoming meetings where they would have an opportunity to discuss the changes. TRINOVA had been offering three funds—multi-asset, government securities and GIC—administered by the company, plus one international and three U.S. equity funds from a major fund family. Krakos says that after merging a large DB plan into the 401(k) in 1993, TRINOVA decided the time had come to turn the entire investment management job over to its mutual fund provider.

A money market fund replaced the old government securities fund, the multi-asset and GIC funds were replaced by look-alikes, the four equity choices remained the same and a corporate bond fund was added.

Meetings on company time for all employees on all shifts in all locations have become a regular feature of TRINOVA's educational program. This series included representatives from the mutual fund company who not only discussed the new fund selections, but also explained what a mutual fund is, historical rates of return, risk versus reward and how compound interest functions as the real force behind meeting long-term financial goals.

After the investment management change went into effect, Krakos and her staff fanned out across the country to repeat the meetings and reinforce the message. They discussed tax advantages of participating in the 401(k), ways to determine how much each employee needed to save and the importance of taking an active role in the management of one's own money and retirement savings.

As 1994 drew to a close, Krakos recorded a rise in 401(k) participation and by the end of 1995, a notable improvement in the diversification of assets. In 1993, before her educational effort began, participation was about 64%. It is now 73%. In 1992, when the first flyer was distributed, 60% of assets were in the GIC fund and another 4% were in the government securities fund. By March 1996, assets in fixed-income investments were down to 47%. Even better, whenever employees designated a different future allocation, only 37% were slated for fixed-income investments.

The Guide That Comes With Most 401(k) Plans.

The Guide That Comes With Ours.

Choose some retirement plans and they'll send you a book. Choose the NationsBank 401(k), on the other hand, and we'll send you a communication consultant: a living, breathing human being who'll explain the program in a way that all your employees will understand.

That's because NationsBank knows that the more informed your employees are about a retirement plan, the more likely they will be to participate. And we've found that there's no better way to ensure their participation than by having someone on site to educate them.

What's more, our communication consultants will return periodically to update your employees and answer any questions they may have. So they'll be able to make wiser decisions regarding their investments as a result.

But what makes the NationsBank 401(k) plan even better is that this communication program is just part of a superior, integrated package that includes administrative and investment services as well.

To learn more about NationsBank call Pamela Hubby at (404)607-4999. And see what a difference having the right guide can make. **NationsBank** Retirement Services

"We don't look at that shift from fixed-income to equities as a stand-alone success," Krakos hastens to say. "Our concern for our employees is, are you in the funds you should be in? Our educational efforts teach people that they should put their money where they want it, but we remind them to *be sure you understand where you put it*. If you have your money in fixed-income, understand that you're not taking as great a risk as you would with equities but you may have to work longer, contribute more and may not reach your financial goal with a 6% annual rate of return. If you are comfortable with that, then fixed-income may be a choice for you."

TAKING EDUCATION A STEP FURTHER

A new, aggressive educational campaign begun in April 1996 is designed to increase that understanding. In a series of two-hour retirement planning seminars, new tools were presented that employees could use to help themselves. Krakos also uses focus groups and surveys to get important employee feedback. Participants have indicated that they want more education and help so they can understand how much they really need to save for retirement.

"Our employees fall into two distinct populations. Those who understand 401(k)s fully and actively manage them are a very small group. The majority can tell you their asset balance and where they're putting their money, but when you ask them whether they should invest in a S&P 500 Index portfolio or a fixed-income fund, they get really nervous."

Krakos hired an outside education provider who had no financial connections and began planning retirement seminars based on a do-it-yourself computer program. Recognizing that many employees do not have computers, every screen in the program was reproduced in a booklet that functions as a series of worksheets so that anyone could go through the program without a computer. Each screen was also presented as a slide and discussed in the meetings. The software is sold for $25, but anyone who doesn't want to buy it can fill out a questionnaire with personal financial information and submit it to the education company to be run through their computer program and mailed back. Employees may do that five times over the next couple of years for the same $25.

Krakos tried out the program in two pilot sessions last year. One of the big issues discussed was how much money people need in order to retire comfortably. "It shocks a lot of people to hear that a 30-year old could need $1 million. 'Oh, I'll never get there,' they say. The fun part is that we show them how to get there— realistically. How much comes out of the paycheck, how that affects current lifestyle, how to fill in the gaps," Krakos says. "People are amazed that someone can reach their retirement goals largely through a 401(k). Then they get excited and say 'I can really do this!'"

The response to the pilot programs was overwhelmingly favorable, according to the post-program surveys. Krakos estimates participation increased about 25% at the two plants and diversification improved as well. To her surprise, everyone bought the software, although later some found they couldn't use it by themselves and were allowed to trade it in for the worksheet alternative.

There is one problem, however. "Once we do this program, we can't stop," Krakos says. "So we need to see how we can incorporate it in future years into a

INVESTORS PRESS
INVITES YOU TO
VISIT OUR WEB SITE...

Learn how you can offer these two important IP
books to your 401(k) administrators and participants:
these books help educate them about their plans.

 **www.investorspress.com**

regular communications strategy which not only brings new hires up to speed but reinforces the message we've been giving existing employees over the years."

There are a few other things on her mind, as well. The controversy over the flat tax concept has employees worried that 401(k) contributions will lose their tax-deferred status. One of the major incentives that gets people to contribute, she points out, is the tax-deferral benefit.

Another concern shared by many employees is the current low limit on tax-deferred contributions to 401(k)s. Not only are there many people who will earn more as the years pass, but because of TRINOVA's generous profit-sharing plan, even low-wage workers must occasionally be given some money in cash to avoid exceeding contribution limits. Krakos thinks that makes no sense at all.

"I want to rest well at night, knowing that we did everything we could to make sure that every one of our employees had everything they needed to live a reasonable life in their retirement years." The strategies TRINOVA has put in place and continues to refine and expand suggest that they may, indeed, achieve that goal.

CHAPTER

TEN

SURVIVING DOWNSIZING:
SOLID PLANNING SUCCEEDS

Westinghouse Savannah River Co.
Aiken, SC

T his is a silver lining story with a reassuring
lesson: even when big things go wrong, a well-
designed education plan can achieve solid results.
Biz Mann, Team Leader, Retirement Services for
Westinghouse Savannah River, produced a 30%
reduction in fixed-income investments in less than a
year even as other parts of her carefully planned program produced disappointing results. What worked,
worked very well. What didn't was the result of bad
luck and bad timing.

In February 1995 Mann began implementing a
massive, long-planned program of employee workshops to introduce changes in mutual fund investment options, some new funds and a new bundled

> Produces nuclear fuel for industry, academic research and the military
> 5 reactors and ancillary facilities over 300 square mile site
> 13,500 employees
> 89% participation rate
> 50 cents-on-the-dollar match up to 6% of salary
> Defined benefit plan
> 401(k) plan assets: $660 million

service provider with an 800-number. An equally important objective was to
increase investment diversification and attract and convert non-participants.

For many years, Westinghouse Savannah had offered five fund options
from three providers: fixed-income, balanced, growth, equity index and asset
allocation funds. Doing all the administration in-house was a growing problem.
The solution was to outsource—but without spending any more money. The
bank that had been doing the recordkeeping was chosen. It offered a respected
name, good investments and good participant services at an affordable price.
But there was a catch: contributions to the most popular equity fund in the old
plan had to be frozen because that fund was not offered by the new vendor.
Participants could leave their money in that fund, they just couldn't contribute
any more.

Many people were very unhappy when they got the letters sent to all employees
at home and at work announcing the changes. However, the change may
have improved attendance at the 248 investment workshops Mann was planning

over six weeks to cover the more than 100 shifts at the various Westinghouse Savannah facilities.

SURVIVING THE STORM OF MASSIVE LAYOFFS: SELLING THE PROGRAM

Advance publicity included posters and announcements in the company newspaper. Information packets were sent to everyone at home and included a booklet describing the new participant service center, the new investment options and new investment selection forms as well as a pre-assigned personal identification number (PIN) for accessing the new service center. Anyone who wanted to change his or her PIN could do so simply by calling the service center once it was up and running. Mann also relied on the company's training staff to help promote the investment workshops, organize the sessions for each facility and sign people up.

Preparations were well underway when the first coincidence of bad timing struck: a week after the workshop sign-up sheets were posted, Westinghouse Savannah announced layoffs of 4,000 of its 18,000 employees. Despite the bad news and its negative impact on the workforce, the workshops had to go on. It would have been extraordinarily difficult to postpone them after coordinating such complicated planning; employees had to be told about the new investment opportunities and the new telephone service line scheduled to start a couple of months later.

Seven new investment choices were being added. The fixed-income and balanced funds remained the same, but Mann was adding mid-cap, small-cap and international equity funds, three asset allocation funds for short-, mid- and long-term horizons, and a well-known growth fund to replace the one being frozen.

PUSHING DIVERSIFICATION

Mann structured the workshops to cover the same information retirement planning sessions would normally include and had them conducted by financial planners from a well-known accounting firm. Materials similar to those sent to employees at home were handed out at the workshops, along with workbooks used to design personal investment strategies. A risk worksheet asked nine questions to determine personal risk tolerance, identify each participant's profile and apply that profile to the choice of subsequent investment options.

The entire package was saturated with color to make the information attractive and easy to follow. The risk profile used gold to blue to brown colored circles to identify conservative, moderate and aggressive profile choices. Three pre-mixed "lifestyle" funds were done in shades of purple, from pale for short-term to deep purple for long-term. A separate retirement planning kit was also color-coded to show what an investment mix might look like for people with various risk tolerances. This was particularly useful after employees calculated their retirement needs and where that money would come from, including Social Security, outside savings and any other money a family might have.

Complicating the education process was Westinghouse Savannah's mixed employee population: there were many Ph.Ds., nuclear engineers and nuclear physicists and large numbers of blue-collar employees. Mann targeted all the materials to an eighth-grade reading level, acknowledging that she risked annoying some and confusing others and noting that, fortunately, educational level is not necessarily indicative of investment knowledge.

Convincing employees to save for retirement can be an uphill battle. Don't fight it alone.

The American Savings Education Council can help. We're a partnership of more than 170 private and public sector organizations—including IBM, Bankers Trust, Fidelity, Employee Benefit Research Institute, Investment Company Institute, U.S. Department of Labor and U.S. Department of the Treasury—dedicated to raising public awareness about the importance of saving and planning for long-term, personal financial independence.

We'd be stronger with your company as a partner. Our brochures, "Top 10 Ways to beat the clock and prepare for retirement" and "The Power to Choose," are available to your company to help you explain saving and retirement planning to your employees.

For information about the American Savings Education Council, please call or write us and visit our web site. The battle for your employees' financial future is on. And we're up for the fight.

ASEC
AMERICAN SAVINGS EDUCATION COUNCIL

American Savings Education Council
Suite 600 · 2121 K Street NW, Washington, DC 20037-1896
Tel: (202) 775-9130 · Fax: (202) 775-6312
Web Site: http://www.asec.org

"Lots of people are totally unaware that because these 401(k) plans are tax-deferred, their money compounds much faster. They get stuck on the negative, that their money is not as readily accessible as it is in a brokerage or savings account," Mann says, so considerable effort was put into explaining the tax advantages of a 401(k), as well as teaching basics, like compounding.

MAKING RISK PERSONAL

Each presentation used a computer program projected onto a screen that allowed various combinations of numbers to be typed in to illustrate different examples—totals changed for 20 years or 30 years to retirement, 6% or 10% contributions. The workshop presenters encouraged people to ask questions during the sessions; they also tried to draw the audience into the program by personalizing the problems and asking questions: "How could you increase your savings rate? How could you close that gap?"

"The presenters were very open about risk and tried to help employees understand the real meaning of loss," Mann says. "They showed how stocks may gain one year, lose one year, then gain for another five years. They showed how the performance of the S&P 500 and aggressive stocks, shown by the small-cap index, evens out over time. They reminded people that when you talk about the risk of loss, you're talking about a snapshot of time—not the long time period for which a retirement plan is meant."

The new investment options were laid against a risk spectrum and their earnings compared over various periods of time so everyone could see that long-term results overshadowed short-term volatility. Mann believes that listing the various mutual funds in a risk sequence like that was particularly effective in demonstrating the importance of diversification as well as the possibilities of mixing and matching within an individual's asset allocation. "We didn't do an intellectual program. We tried to see how people feel," Mann says. "What they are really scared of is that fluctuation. We know because if the market goes down, people sell."

The presentations included what Mann calls "gut checks," or guidance on how to deal with emotional nervousness even though you understand rationally that there is no need to be nervous. The recommendation was to start by diversifying slowly, putting 10% or 20% of assets into a stock fund and watching it for a year or two, then adding more gradually, with no need to jump in. Every member of every audience was encouraged to fill out the new investment selection forms right there in the meeting and hand them in on their way out the door, a tactic Mann considers particularly useful. For those who chose not to do so, the information packets included a postage-paid return envelope.

MEASURING RESULTS

The workshops produced a stunning improvement in diversification but other results were disappointing. Before the workshops, Mann says 67% of the 401(k) plan's money was in the fixed-income fund. A month after the new investments became available, that number had dropped to 59% and it kept going down. Over the next ten months, the number dropped another 12 points to its current 47%.

"Having somebody speaking right in front of you, a real person, made the difference," Mann says, although she also gives credit for some of the recent improvement in diversification to the lure of the stock market's exceptional performance in 1995.

But after all the planning, work, mailings and handouts, articles in the company newspaper, posters and promotions at each site facility, Mann was disappointed that only 55% of the employees attended the workshops, even though they were held on company time. She blames the unfortunate timing that pitted her investment seminars against layoff notices.

Not only was attendance at the workshops disappointing, there was hardly an increase in participation. Given Westinghouse Savannah's already high participation rate, Mann had not expected much improvement, but she had certainly hoped for even small signs that eligible enrollees were entering the fold. Nonetheless, Mann is undeterred. She wants to do the whole thing over again, but better. "What I'm concerned about is having a market correction without our employees having had any additional education."

An Internal Cost of Outsourcing

One of the results of outsourcing, however, was that management concluded that Mann's department no longer needed its staff. She tried to hold on to enough people to keep the education program moving forward but was able, finally, to keep only one person.

"It wasn't as if one day all the employees started calling the service center," she notes. "The first three months we got almost the same number of daily calls as we did before we outsourced, but I'd gone from eight people down to one. So, we've been taking care of the problems associated with the transition to outsourcing and we haven't had time to do the kind of educational follow-up that I think really matters."

An Eye to the Future

With the transition now complete and the program running smoothly, Mann is finally finding the time to look ahead. She estimates it will take five or six months to put together a comprehensive educational program with so little staff support. She is thinking about offering a new series of workshops as part of the regular weekly or monthly staff meetings at each site facility, rather than asking employees to take time out for separate investment workshops. That would offer the added benefits of a captive audience and give her a way to reach almost every single employee.

Mann is also considering utilizing the new human resources service centers at some of the site facilities where employees could be invited to attend brown-bag luncheon seminars on saving and investing. "I'd like to do the whole nine yards and that would mean more than one session. It could be three or four on retirement planning, financial planning, the basics, the plan itself. We could gear one seminar to people who are savers, one to people who are investors and want to get into alpha, beta and more sophisticated stuff," Mann says with determination.

Bad luck and bad timing may have dimmed the luster of Mann's efforts, but significantly higher diversification alone is no small accomplishment. Westinghouse Savannah's longtime commitment to education is firmly in place and Mann is ready to capitalize on what she has learned from disappointment as well as success.

TIPS FROM THE TRENCHES:
101 SOLUTIONS TO PROBLEMS IN 401(k)
COMMUNICATIONS AND EDUCATION

TIPS FROM THE TRENCHES is a Special Section that can help you make your 401(k) plan communications and education efforts more successful. It brings together a cross section of the nation's best thinking from plan administrators who are directly involved in the daily management of 401(k)s and providers who anticipate, understand and meet their needs as they educate America's growing number of plan participants and eligible enrollees.

- Smart Pill
- Tip from Plan Sponsor
- Tip from Provider
- Tip from this Book

Assembled for the first time in one easy-to-use reference resource, **TIPS FROM THE TRENCHES** offers 101 easy-to-implement ideas you can use to solve day-to-day plan management problems.

The first tip, from a 401(k) provider, is one that all plan administrators should remember when the challenge of communicating with employees and educating plan participants seems daunting. It may be the most important tip of all:

1. Relax. Don't try to solve every problem all at once. Focus on one problem at a time—such as raising participation rates at the Chicago plant or increasing equity investments for employees under 40—and monitor your success with measurable results.

The most effective communications and education programs are developed and implemented logically, step by step. Don't expect that you can or will increase contribution levels or improve asset allocation for employees at all ages, levels and locations with a single effort—success has to be measured one triumph at a time.

IP's Editors

I. HOW TO INCREASE PARTICIPATION IN YOUR COMPANY'S 401(k) PLAN

Alleviate Fear of Investment Loss

2 Employees are worried about losing their money. Recognize that fear of investment loss is human nature, but acceptance of risk can be learned. Educate your employees about the different kinds of investment risk.

3 Emphasize that although there are risks attached to everything we do—especially making investment decisions—long-term benefits often outweigh short-term risks.

4 Don't simply parrot conventional wisdom about investing. Acknowledge employees' real life concerns and fears: tell them you understand how frightening it is to think they may not have enough money to live on after a lifetime of work.

5 Redefine risk for employees to mean *the probability of not meeting your retirement objectives*.

6 Emphasize that it can be too risky to be too safe—*the biggest risk may be taking no risk at all*.

7 Point out that loss in a fund is real *only when you make a withdrawal*.

8 Create volatility models for employees that illustrate how their investment risk fluctuates.

9 Westinghouse Savannah presents plan investment options within a risk spectrum and compares the earnings of each over various periods of time to illustrate that long-term results overshadow short-term volatility.

10 Explain that the real risk is not to lose money in the short-term, but to end up without enough money for the long-term.

11 Encourage realistic expectations. Employees, like everyone else, are most comfortable when they know what to expect and can make decisions based on realistic probabilities.

12 Help employees make investment decisions that meet their "sleep factor"—choosing investment risks that won't keep them up at night.

● PLAN SPONSOR ● PROVIDER ● BOOK

Use Employee Testimonials

 J.P. Morgan uses actual employee testimonials in its educational materials; they help generate employee buy-in to the plan.

 Illinois-based Household International features actual retirees in its company magazine who share their thoughts on retirement planning and make powerful comments, such as "Without the 401(k), I wouldn't be in the secure position I am today."

Use Targeted Solicitations

 Recognize that many different demographic groups usually exist in any one company, but there are only two major categories of employees: those who want to learn and those who don't.

 Arizona-based Microchip Technology's discretionary semi-annual matching contribution is based on company profitability. The company sends participants notification of the company match every six months. In 1995, to increase participation, they began sending non-participants "no match" notifications, a memo highlighting what they *could have* contributed over the last six months, saved in taxes and gained from the company match.

 Similarly, at tax time J.P. Morgan sends "deadbeat letters" to non-participants that show how big a tax deduction they are handing back to Uncle Sam.

 New Jersey-based Bellcore also believes in letting Uncle Sam help tout the benefits of the plan. Bellcore sends out notices at tax time each year reminding employees that they can reduce the tax bite on their salaries by contributing (or contributing more) to the 401(k) plan. Notices are sent as an insert in quarterly statements, in the company newsletter and via E-mail.

 If employees waive participation, Household International sends them a letter listing projected savings for the next 5, 10 and 15 years. Employees who stop contributing get a reminder that for only the cost of a fast-food burger and fries they can rejoin the plan. Those who suspend contributions due to a hardship withdrawal are reminded they are eligible to participate in the plan again. Targeted letters have increased participation by 12%.

 Produce a plan statement for *non-participating* employees that gives them an example of how the 401(k) works. Make it simple.

Emphasize the Portability of the 401(k)

 To combat employee concerns about recent or possible corporate downsizing, emphasize that with the 401(k), you *can* take it with you.

Overcome the Misconception That Employees Can't Afford to Save

Pennsylvania's Air Products and Chemicals stresses that regardless of their income level, employees become accustomed to living on their paycheck. That's why their employees are eligible for the 401(k) as soon as they're hired. Employees are given one-on-one counseling during orientation and encouraged to sign up before they receive their first paycheck—or have a chance to say they can't afford to save. The participation rate among new hires is 80%.

J.P. Morgan chronicles how much the average person spends on odds and ends on a typical day to illustrate how easy it is to cut out non-essentials and save money instead.

Help Lower-Salaried Employees Start to Save

Illinois-based GLS Corporation acknowledges that most employees are focused on take-home pay rather than gross pay. GLS shows its employees that because of tax benefits, they can put 1% or 2% of their gross salary in the 401(k) plan and end up with the *same* take-home pay they would have if they had contributed nothing.

To make the point that young employees should put some of their spending money into the 401(k), Sleepeck Printing in Illinois created two paychecks for each employee: one in the amount of their current take home pay and the other showing the amount they *would* take home if they contributed 10% to the plan.

Sleepeck held special meetings where employees discussed the amount they could switch each week from expenses to contributions and how much money they would save by age 65 if they made those changes. The company discovered that many employees did not have checking accounts and were paying several dollars every week to cash checks. These employees were taught how to open bank accounts—a simple but powerful tool to help them save. The result: 88% of the target group enrolled in the plan.

Save Mart, a California-based supermarket chain, created a series of payroll stuffers focused on ordinary things young employees spend money on each week. It showed employees the growth potential of that money saved for various periods of time. One week they featured the five-day cost of a candy bar and a soda: the total was at least 1% of a young employee's salary. Other weeks they featured cigarettes and videos. This tactic made a big impression, especially when employees saw that by starting early even a small regular contribution would add up to hundreds of thousands of dollars in 30 years.

Sterile Concepts emphasizes to lower-paid employees that they should not be embarrassed to save just 1% of their salaries. An important message is repeated: every dollar counts toward retirement.

● PLAN SPONSOR   ● PROVIDER   ● BOOK

29 Coors made it as easy as possible for employees to join the plan by eliminating unnecessary and cumbersome restrictions, such as limiting the number of times a year a participant can change contribution amounts or transfer assets from one fund to another.

30 Recognize the power of peer influence and try to target "King Pin" employees like union representatives or department heads, who can get the attention of their co-workers and help spread your message.

Attract Participants With Technology

31 Apple Computer's company-wide web site lets employees click on for whatever enrollment form they need and bring it up on their own screen. They can fill it out and send it directly to the benefits department. Employees love the system, calling it fun and easier to use than anything previously available.

32 The University of Pennsylvania set up kiosks with remote video and computer links to its provider. It allowed eligible employees to make appointments to speak with real counselors who led them through a retirement planning package that showed projections and strategies based on individual circumstances. The counselor's face was always visible on the screen's video window throughout the session. After considerable positive feedback, the University plans to offer this service each year during an annual retirement planning event.

Produce Individual Benefit Statements That Project Retirement Income From All Sources

33 Springs Window in Wisconsin found that despite the fact that they do not offer a company match, when they produced individual benefit statements for each employee that projected income from Social Security, the profit-sharing plan and potential 401(k) savings, the need to save hit home and participation increased by 10%.

34 Sterile Concepts warns employees that they cannot necessarily depend on Social Security.

Make Savings Benefits Concrete

35 Alcoa uses real money—a shiny new 50 cent piece—attached to one of its communications to drive home the point that participants will get a 50 cent match for every dollar they contribute.

Lure Participants With "Free Money"

36 IBM uses the provocative headline, "Are you getting your free money yet?" on the cover of a colorful enrollment flyer designed to lure new hires into the 401(k) plan. The flyer describes the company match of 50 cents-on-the-dollar up to 6% of salary as an automatic 50% return on your investment.

Appeal to Both Decision-Makers

Alcoa, American Stores and TRINOVA all follow the same golden rule: They mail enrollment information to employees' homes so that spouses and other family memebers can be involved in the decision-making process.

Hold special investment and retirement planning meetings after work hours and invite spouses and other family members.

Get Employees to Buy-In to the Plan

To increase employee buy-in to the plan and build a company-wide "team" attitude, The Homer D. Bronson Company ties the company match to company performance in achieving strategic goals.

To make employees feel they have a real stake in their company, Kendall Packaging Corp. developed a match based on company profits that makes employees feel as though they are shareholders.

To increase employee morale and performance, Kendall initiated a direct dialogue between management and line workers through a series of meetings that shows employees that their grievances are heard, understood and responded to by management.

Be Smart With Your Education Dollars

42 Alcoa says that when you outsource you must stay involved: schedule weekly status calls that keep you informed and proactive.

43 Plan an annual calendar for your communications that maximizes the use of your available financial and human resources.

44 To centralize plan resources and reduce communications mailing costs, North Dakota-based Lake Region Clinic is building a reference library in the employee lounge where employees can borrow books and videos on retirement and investment planning.

45 When Coors offers an educational book or another free plan "give-away," the company mails only a descriptive coupon to employees at home and asks them to stop by the benefits department to pick it up.

Get Employees to Read What You Send Them

46 Focus your communications on the investors and their needs, not on the investments.

47 Ask participants which topics they want more information on; get employee feedback and use it as your craft your communications program.

48 The New York-based American Society of Composers and Producers (ASCAP) agrees and devised a simple strategy: employees are asked what they *will* read. After discovering that their employees didn't know they had a Summary Plan Description and swore they never read it, focus groups convinced the director of human resources to send memos or E-mail with "IMPORTANT: ABOUT YOUR 401(k)" headlines and content focused clearly on only one point at a time.

49 Consider the "investor psychology" of each employee group in your company as you prepare and target your communications.

50 Household International sends weekly E-mail messages to all employees explaining single concepts, such as dollar cost averaging or the magic of compounding. It also launched a series of newsletters that focus on one topic at a time.

51 When a survey revealed that NYNEX employees loved their retirement program but didn't really understand it, the company realized that their deferral to a very cautious legal department had resulted in communications that were mired in confusing "lawyer lingo". NYNEX hired a public relations professional who had no benefits background to rewrite everything they sent out from the benefits department. "They used to call me the mushroom because their strategy was to keep me in the dark," the writer says of his job to translate educational materials into English, making them short and simple, and easy to "sell".

 To make sure that Calspan SRL Corporation's New York-based scientists pay attention to plan communications, the company developed "the science of retirement-based investing", a tag line for all materials. A puzzle is available which, after it is assembled, explains plan benefits and invitations. Employee meetings use familiar lingo and compare the three laws of motion to the three laws of investing: start early, save regularly and monitor your results.

Relate Investing to the Rest of the World

 In quarterly performance reports, Alcoa includes outside news developments that may affect future performance of funds.

Kendall Packaging Corp. uses company bulletin boards to post national news events affecting the company's 401(k).

Know Your Audience

Coors creates communications for three different groups of employees: those who are not contributing the maximum amount; those who are invested only in the fixed-income fund; those who are investing the maximum and are well-diversified.

Westinghouse Savannah feels that a person's educational level is not necessarily indicative of his or her investment knowledge: the company gears its communications to an eighth-grade reading level for all employees.

Sterile Concepts offers education programs in several languages and uses simple English in communications in order to reach the company's bilingual workforce.

Reinforce Your Message

 TRINOVA continually stresses the tax advantages of plan participation, how much money employees need for retirement and the importance of managing one's own money and financial future.

Don't Underestimate Your Employees

 American Stores believes that people in the ranks *can* absorb complex information: delivering the facts helps employees draw good conclusions—but present the information so they can understand it.

● PLAN SPONSOR   ● PROVIDER   ● BOOK

60) Organize employee meetings around subjects and levels of investment knowledge: don't assume all senior executives know more than every factory worker or secretary. You can repackage the same investment information so that it appeals to people of higher and lower levels of investment sophistication, regardless of their job title.

Think of Your Plan as a Product: Win Consumer Attention and Dollars

61) Coors applies inexpensive advertising concepts to simple ideas—the TERA Turtle is now widely recognized and accepted as the company's 401(k) mascot.

62) Borrowing from traditional billboard advertising, American Stores puts posters and table-tents in the employee lunchrooms that focus on a single, different topic each quarter.

63) J.P. Morgan recommends keeping the visuals in videos familiar and personal—shoot scenes in the local neighborhood employees recognize and use real employees instead of actors.

64) In J.P. Morgan's plan communications, the emphasis is on how people *feel* about issues and react to information, rather than how they *think* about them. Humor is also a key: if people feel they are being entertained as well as informed, they are more apt to absorb important information.

Keep High-Tech Human

65) Alcoa instituted a telephone voice response system with 24-hour, 800-number access—and personalized the technology by using real people at the other end of the call.

66) Sterile Concepts doesn't assume that their 24-hour 800-number is a no-brainer for all employees. If callers are confused, the human resource department is available to help by walking them through the steps of the answer.

67) Apple Computer logs all the calls to its help lines so it can analyze if the communications and education program is eliminating confusion, not adding to it.

68) TRINOVA suggests using a do-it-yourself computer program that shows employees how much money they need to retire. It also shows them how big a contribution the 401(k) makes to a total amount that is, inevitably, a shocking sum for anybody.

69) Apple Computer transferred all employee benefit information to an internal web site cross-linked to the mutual funds in the 401(k) plan, the medical insurer and other key service providers so that employees can access the information they want easily, whenever they want it. The company was careful to make the system easy and fun to use.

Position Your Investment Manager as a Valuable Employee Resource

70 PHS, Inc., the Connecticut-based physicians health service, invites all employees to meet with its investment manager at a 45-minute group meeting. 80% attend. The investment manager is positioned as a valuable and accessible resource, available to individual employees to discuss the funds and answer investment questions over the phone, as well.

Help Employees Overcome Investment Inertia

71 To discourage employees from choosing money market funds, Virginia-based Science Applications International Corporation (SAIC), the largest employee-owned research and development company in the world, introduced life strategy funds as an alternative investment option. For those who choose not to choose, these funds help employees determine their risk tolerance and increase their diversification quickly and easily.

72 Many of Save Mart's supermarket baggers can't calculate percentages and don't understand how to compute their savings over time, but they are afraid to ask questions or appear ignorant. To battle self-consciousness and math phobia, the company supplies investment counselors with simple, easy-to-read charts that show the exact amount of a 1%, 2% and 3% deferral for each employee.

73 Since employees often view their 401(k) payroll deductions as "take aways", Household International reinforces the benefits of the plan in short messages on payroll stubs.

74 TRINOVA believes that you should tell employees to put their money wherever they want it—but you should help them understand the advantages, disadvantages and consequences of their investment choices.

75 To help employees understand their investment options fully, Kendall Packaging Corp. asks its fund company to provide a monthly report listing each fund's performance as part of the company's communications program.

76 Save Mart targets employees who have little understanding of why they should diversify out of the money market fund by using the analogy of paying for credit. In small group meetings employees are asked how much interest they are paying for car loans, mortgages and credit card purchases. Then they are told: "You mean you are willing to pay somebody else 10% for your car loan, but you are only willing to pay yourself 5% in the money market fund?" The message gets across.

● PLAN SPONSOR ● PROVIDER ● BOOK

To help employees understand compounding, the company explains that mortgage interest illustrates compound earning in reverse. When you take out a 30-year, $100,000 mortgage, the interest you pay compounds and eventually you pay over $300,000 to the bank. Employees are usually stunned to realize this, but it successfully illustrates the idea of compounding over long periods.

Stress the Importance of Asset Allocation

 Point out that many professional money managers believe that asset allocation may account for as much as 90% of investment returns. Focus your message on asset allocation, not individual fund choices.

 Encourage employees to minimize overall market risk through gradual asset allocation shifts and periodic portfolio rebalancing.

 Show employees how important diversification is: explain how it can mitigate risk over the long-term.

 Illustrate how plan costs—both obvious and hidden—impact investment return.

Encourage Total Financial Planning

 IBM reimburses its employees up to $250 per year for the cost of getting a personal financial plan from either of two designated financial service firms. The company calls it financial wellness. "The way you manage your financial wellness is to have periodic check-ups with your financial planner to make sure you're investing wisely." In the program's first two years, more than 15,000 financial plans were purchased.

Put Risk in its Proper Perspective

 Describe inflation as "the hidden risk" and show employees how they can beat it.

 To encourage employees to take on more risk, Air Products and Chemicals explains that with benefits from the company DB plan and Social Security, their 401(k) assets represent only 30% to 40% of their total retirement income. So even if all of their 401(k) money goes into a higher-risk vehicle, only about one-third of their total retirement money is at higher risk.

 To help employees understand the real meaning of investment "loss", Westinghouse Savannah explains that the risk of loss usually refers to a "snapshot" of time rather than the life of the retirement plan.

 Demonstrate the risk of losing money over various time periods for different asset classes.

86 Focus on the frequency of quarters with a negative return to demonstrate the relative volatility of investments.

87 Show recovery periods after significant market corrections.

88 Don't explain the risk in an investment vehicle based on a single summary quantitative measure or rating.

89 Help employees recognize the risk of applying pre-retirement investment strategies to post-retirement financial planning.

90 Explain the critical importance of understanding how to take retirement distributions.

Generate Maximum Interest in Employee Meetings: Before, During and After

91 Emphasize that if employees *don't attend* special retirement planning meetings, they'll get nothing out of them.

92 Use proven promotional techniques to get employees to attend meetings: advertise heavily, promise give-aways, use eye-catching themes and incent intermediaries (regional human resource staff) to promote the event.

93 Charge $1.00 for employees to attend meetings, but commit to an immediate return on their investment by the meeting's end—$1.25 in the case of a plan with a 25% match.

94 Offer treats—ice cream sundaes, lunch or breakfast, coffee and cookies—to increase attendance. Food works.

95 Make the meetings mandatory and have a strong management presence.

96 Keep the human resources people in the field up-to-date so they can tell employees what they can expect to learn in advance. Before quarterly enrollment meetings, Household International sends out a leader's guide to all HR people focusing on key points to be covered and including overheads and handouts.

97 Stress that the meetings will not be lectures and encourage employees to participate in interactive, in-depth Q&A sessions.

98 To keep employees' attention during meetings, J.P. Morgan varies the pace and delivery of information by using different presentation methods (videos, slides and presenters).

99 Research shows that only 10% of new information is remembered within 48 hours of a presentation. To raise retention rates, use everyday language and examples

● PLAN SPONSOR   ● PROVIDER   ● BOOK

and encourage participants not to "take" notes during the meetings, but to "make" notes so they absorb what they are learning and apply it to their own retirement planning. Some plan sponsors distribute prepared notes with fill-in-the-blank sections.

 To boost retention rates, engage participants in an ongoing program that capitalizes on adult learning techniques, such as providing opportunities for employees to problem-solve with their peers.

 Target different audiences for different meetings. Coors holds basic investment meetings for non-participants and those saving less than the maximum and other meetings to cover advanced investment concepts for sophisticated investors.

American Express Financial Advisors Inc.

P.O. Box 489, Minneapolis, MN 55440-0489

Key Contacts:

American Express
    Institutional Services 1-800-437-0600
(*A division of American Express Financial Advisors Inc.*)
Ward Armstrong, *Sr. Vice President* .. 612-671-1915

Year Founded 1894

Assets Under Management:

	Clients	Assets
Total American Express Financial Advisors Inc.	1.9M	$138B
American Express Institutional Services	464**	$11.5B*
Custodial Assets		$71.1B*

 * As of 6/30/96; asset figures for American Express Trust Company
** Corporate/Institutional clients

Special Areas of Expertise:

American Express Institutional Services, a division of American Express Financial Advisors Inc., along with American Express Trust Company, offers the complete defined contribution/401(k) plan out-sourcing solution—from investments, trust and recordkeeping to employee education. American Express Financial Advisors offers a range of mutual fund products to both institutional and retail clients, all developed and managed to represent the various risk/return steps on the investment spectrum. American Express Trust Company provides collective funds specifically designed for qualified plans and managed in compliance with ERISA. American Express Trust Company also provides separate stable capital account management services. Access to outside money management is available to qualified plan investors through SmartPartners[SM] alliance.

Investment Approach:

For all our disciplines, our investment philosophy is consistent with our 102-year history. We believe our approach is well suited to the needs of retirement plan sponsors and participants. By consistently applying the disciplined, hands-on management skills acquired through more than 50 years in fund management, American Express Financial Advisors seeks to manage investments without exposing plan participants to more near-term volatility than is necessary to seek to achieve the investment objective.

Diversified Investment Advisors

Four Manhattanville Road, Purchase, NY 10577
Phone 800-770-6797 • Fax 914-697-3743

Key Contact:

James G. Russell, VP– Investment Marketing

The Firm:

Diversified offers comprehensive programs of high-quality investments and administrative services to Defined Benefit, Defined Contribution and Not-for-Profit plan sponsors. Diversified forms a partnership with its clients to provide exceptional investment management, plan design, participant communication programs, recordkeeping services and technical guidance.

Total Retirement Assets Under Management:
$9.2 Billion

Discretionary Assets Under Management:
$1.1 Billion

Investment Philosophy:

Diversified's investment approach is founded on four fundamental principles:
- Performance is overwhelmingly influenced by strategic asset allocation.
- Asset allocation requires a broad array of funds representing major asset classes.
- Efficient investing through asset allocation demands specialized expertise in managing assets to strict investment objectives. Diversified achieves this through the selection of highly accomplished, independent investment managers.
- Continuous monitoring of each manager is essential to assure strict adherence to the investment objective of each asset class.

Special Qualified Plan Features:

- Customized asset allocation advisory service.
- Access to a full spectrum of investment options, managed by 17 independent money management firms utilizing 34 portfolio managers.
- Diversified's 401(k) Service Guarantee.
- Diversified's 403(b) "Audit Proof" Program
- Access to a full range of self-directed investment options, including individual stocks and bonds as well as over 800 mutual funds through Charles Schwab & Co. Inc.

Fidelity Investments®

82 Devonshire Street, Boston, MA 02109

Key Contacts:

Fidelity Institutional Retirement Services Company
(FIRSCO) 1-800-343-9184
Peter Smail, *President* 508-787-8090
Ray Marcinowski, *Sr. Vice President* . . 606-386-4001

FIRSCO

Assets Under Management . . . . $111.4 Billion
Number of Clients 5,765
Number of Participants . . . . 3.8 million

Fidelity Institutional Retirement Services Company is the nation's number one provider of 401(k) retirement plans and services in the U.S. FIRSCO provides a comprehensive and integrated solution for retirement plans that makes the lives of plan administrators and participants simpler and more rewarding. All the people and technology that touch your plan work for Fidelity—nothing is outsourced.

For small to mid-sized companies, FIRSCO has a separate business unit that understands and is dedicated to serving 401(k) needs for these particular companies.

Recordkeeping: FIRSCO will invest about $50 million this year in technology. State-of-the-art systems ensure speed and accuracy, thus freeing up our people to proactively consult and anticipate your needs.

Employee Education: Utilizing consumer research, our goal is to understand your participant and to create a targeted communications program that gets results. We provide an extremely comprehensive ongoing education program, including: The Stages Program, Participant Services Group and Internet capabilities.

Investment Management: Research-driven security selection and hiring the most talented mutual fund managers and analysts are two keys to our investment approach. Fidelity offers a large selection of investment options from the Fidelity Fund Family, as well as outside funds through FundsNet partners.

John Hancock Funds

A Global Investment Management Firm

101 Huntington Avenue, Boston, MA 02199
Fax: 617-375-4710

Institutional Investments & Services

Key Contacts:

James V. Bowhers, *Executive VP*   617-375-4880
Edward J. Lavelle, *First VP*   617-375-4706

Organization:

John Hancock Funds is a wholly owned subsidiary of John Hancock Financial Services, one of the nation's leading financial services providers. With more than $44 billion in institutional assets under management, John Hancock has been a leader in the institutional marketplace for over 50 years.

John Hancock Funds' Institutional Investments & Services Group offers a full range of investment management and client services for institutional investors, including institutional mutual funds and separate account management.

Investment Approach:

Disciplined investing using in-depth fundamental research, specializing in:

Equity management
- Growth
- International
- Sector approach
- Value
- Small-capitalization

Fixed-income management
- Global and domestic
- Stable value products

Service Approach:

- Investment Education and Communication Programs
- Daily Valuation Recordkeeping and Plan Administration
- Investment Management and Client Services
- Plan Design and Compliance
- Benefit Payment Services
- Trustee Services
- Investment Advisory Services

KeyCorp

127 Public Square, Cleveland, OH 44114
Phone 216-689-0391 • Fax 216-689-3744
Toll Free 800-982-3811

Key Contacts:
Ann Leuth, *Product Manager* 216-689-0391
Timothy J. Connors, *Sales Manager* . 216-689-5182

Total assets under management: $35B*
401(k) assets managed: $8B*
DC assets managed: $20B*
as of 12/31/95

Our daily valued 401(k) product is PRISM®, which offers the convenience of fully integrated sevices from a single, highly skilled source. This unique management program is designed specifically for 401(k) plans. Multifaceted in concept and design, PRISM provides a total spectrum of services, including investment management, trusteeship and administration services, participant recordkeeping and ongoing employee communication programs.

PRISM offers daily valuation of assets, diversification of investments and increased flexibility in the movement of money. It also features Trust Talk®, an automated telephone inquiry service that relieves the benefit manager from serving as the participant's prime source of information.

To achieve maximum return, we combine the capabilities of our portfolio managers with the advisory expertise of our entire trust and investment management organization. In addition to our proprietary Victory Funds, we also offer outside mutual fund offerings from Fidelity Advisor, Templeton and American Funds.

Working through their own Relationship Manager, our clients can access the resources of more than 100 investment professionals, including Society Asset Management, Inc., KeyCorp's leading registered investment adviser subsidiary, which has one of the largest equity research departments in the nation and more than a dozen fixed-income specialists.

MetLife

One Madison Avenue, New York, NY 10010

Key Contact:
Gary E. Lineberry, *Vice President* 212-578-3181

Total Tax-Exempt Assets Under Management from All Sources $83.8B*
Total Defined Contribution Assets $35B*
as of 12/31/95

Wholly Owned Investment Management Subsidiaries:
State Street Research & Management Company actively manages equity and fixed-income assets for individual and institutional separate accounts and mutual funds. GFM International Investors, Ltd., London, specializes in active non-U.S. equity and fixed-income management of separate account and mutual fund products.

Outside Fund Flexibility:
Diversity in management philosophy and style is made available to both plan sponsors and participants through the MetSelect Alliance℠ and our self-directed brokerage account option. Specifically, our MetSelect Alliance℠ provides access to funds from Founders Asset Management, Inc., Janus Capital Corporation, Neuberger&Berman Management Inc., Scudder, Stevens & Clark, Inc., Twentieth Century Mutual Funds and Warburg, Pincus Counsellors, Inc. In addition, our partnership with The New England affords sponsors access to Loomis Sayles & Company, L.P., Oakmark Funds, and Reich & Tang Capital Management Group. For even more flexibility, our self-directed brokerage account affords participant access to our 2,000 mutual funds plus stocks and bonds listed on major exchanges.

Additional Offerings:
The MetLife/UAM program is designed to deliver institutional investment management services and pricing to large defined contribution plans. A select group of UAM affiliates provide investment management of the equity options in this program. In addition to its role as the provider of integrated services with an emphasis on participant communicatons, MetLife also provides investment management services for the fixed-income and stable value options.

NationsBank

100 North Tryon Street, Charlotte, NC 28255

Key Contact:

Pamela J. Hubby, *SVP*

Retirement Services Sales   404-607-4999

The Company: NationsBank Corporation, the parent company of NationsBank, N.A. ("NationsBank"), is currently the fifth largest bank holding company in the U.S. With over 62,000 professionals, NationsBank and its banking affiliates serve more than 10 million retail households and 600,000 business customers in all aspects of financial services.

Retirement Services: A wide array of retirement plans is available through NationsBank, including 401(k) plans providing unique solutions to customer needs. In addition to investment management, administrative, document and trustee services, NationsBank provides plan sponsors with a comprehensive communication program that helps participants understand the risks of long-term investing and how to determine optimal risk/reward profiles based on their individual needs. NationsBank currently administers over $116 billion in institutional assets for over 3,500 plans nationwide.

Investment Expertise: Since 1874, NationsBank and its predecessors have provided prudent investment management and trust services to individuals, institutions, foundations and endowments. The mutual fund family advised by NationsBank ranks among the top five bank-advised mutual funds based on asset size, and it is the 28th largest fund complex out of 615 bank- and nonbank-affiliated fund families. Forty-four mutual fund portfolios total over $18.5 billion in assets under management.

Plan Sponsor and Participant Services:

NationsBank provides retirement plan services designed to simplify the role of the plan sponsor and encourage a high level of participation among employees. Our expertise in sponsor and participant services includes:

- Plan enrollment documentation and services
- Accurate recordkeeping, maintenance and administrative services
- Timely statements and reporting procedures
- Customized employee communications
- Educational materials
- Enrollment and educational seminars

Neuberger&Berman Management Inc.

605 Third Avenue, New York, NY 10158

Key Contacts:

N&B Management Institutional Services

Peter Sundman, *Senior Vice President* 212-476-8924

Susan Walsh, *Assistant Vice President,*
    Institutional Services 212-476-8928

Dan Dumont, *Vice President,*
    National Director 212-476-8856

Year Founded:

Neuberger&Berman 1939

Neuberger&Berman Management Inc. 1970

Assets Under Management:

Total Neuberger&Berman . . . . $ 40.8 Billion

N&B Management Mutual Funds . . . $ 12.8 Billion

N&B Pension
    Endowment/Institutional . . . . $ 16.5 Billion

N&B High Net Worth . . . . $ 11.5 Billion

About Our Firm: Neuberger&Berman Management Inc. is the investment manager, administrator and distributor of a family of equity and fixed-income no-load mutual funds, including funds used in insurance company products.

Focus on 401(k)s: Our Institutional Department is dedicated to servicing plan sponsors in the 401(k) and defined contribution markets. In addition to providing investment options for qualified plans, Neuberger&Berman Management also provides employee education, enrollment meetings and plan sponsor support. Since 1993, Neuberger&Berman Management has completed over 30 alliance relationships with administrators who service plans ranging in size from fewer than 100 to more than 25,000 participants.

Investment Approach: Each of our equity funds follow one of two basic investment approaches: value or growth. Most of our equity fund portfolio managers pursue the value approach, believing that, over time, undervalued securities are most likely to appreciate in price and be subject to less risk of price decline than securities whose market prices have already reached their perceived economic value. With our fixed-income funds, we follow a similarly limited-risk approach, seeking high total returns consistent with minimal risk to capital.

NYL Benefit Services Company, Inc.

A New York Life Company
846 University Avenue
Norwood, MA 02062-2641

505 Sansome Street, Suite 1701
San Francisco, CA 94111

Key Contacts:
NYL Benefit Services Company:
Joel M. Disend, *President* 617-440-2000
Chris M. Blair, *Vice President,*
　　 Western Region 415-956-1155
Jane Wallace, *Executive Assistant* 800-586-1413

Year Founded:
NYL Benefit Services Company
(formerly ADQ, Inc.) 1970
New York Life 1845

Assets Under Management:*
New York Life Insurance Company and affiliates
Consolidated Assets . . . . $76.4 Billion
*as of 6/30/96

Special Areas of Expertise:
NYL Benefit Services provides a complete range
of retirement plan and benefit consulting services,
including a bundled 401(k) program—401(k)
Complete^{SM}. A full spectrum of mutual funds is
available through NYLIFE Securities Inc., member
NASD, including MainStay Institutional Funds,
Inc. Guaranteed products, including the Pooled
Stable Value Account, as well as Separate Accounts,
are offered by triple-A rated** New York Life
Insurance Company.

*** Independent services rate companies on a number of
factors, including financial strength and claims-paying
ability. Several of the leading services gave New York
Life their highest rating—Moody's Investors Service:
Aaa, based on financial strength; Standard & Poor's
and Duff & Phelps Corporation: AAA for claims-
paying ability; and A.M. Best Company, Inc.: A++
(Superior) for financial strength. These ratings apply
to New York Life Insurance Company, not to any
investment products offered by the company.*

Prudential Retirement Services
30 Scranton Office Park, Moosic, PA 18507

Key Contact Information:
Robert E. Lee, *Vice President, Marketing
& Communications Group* 717-341-6005

Total Assets Under Management From
All Prudential Sources:
as of 12/31/95 . . . . $314 Billion
Defined Contribution Assets:
as of 12/31/95 . . . . $36 Billion
Reporting of Valuation: . . . . Daily
Minimum Account Size: . . . . None

You know us—Prudential has been keeping its
promise of serving investors' financial needs for over
120 years. We are one of the world's leading providers
of diversified financial services and manage $314 billion
in investments for institutional investors, retail investors
and policyholders. Our operations are secured by a
capital base of $11.4 billion. Prudential investment
units manage over $36 billion of defined contribution
assets for public, private and non-profit organizations
through an outstanding family of equity, fixed-income
and balanced investment options. Prudential's client
list includes one out of three FORTUNE 500 companies. More than 14,000 clients trust us to manage their
pension and institutional funds.

We know you—With 68 years of specialized retirement plan expertise, we offer an array of products and
services designed to give your plan participants the
power to live their retirement dreams by:
- Understanding your business environment—through
  a team of dedicated retirement service professionals
- Learning your priorities and concerns—by being at
  your location when *you* need us
- Effectively communicating with you and your
  participants—through award-winning investment
  education materials
- Meeting your current expectations—with our
  advanced recordkeeping system that integrates
  image processing, daily valuation and a voice
  response telephone system
- Anticipating your future needs—we are commited
  to being a leader in the retirement services industry.

Rogers, Casey & Associates, Inc.

One Parklands Drive, Darien, CT 06820
Phone 203-656-5900 • Fax 203-656-2233

Key Contact:

Kenneth G. Rogers
Managing Director, Marketing   203-656-5940

Year Founded: 1976; wholly owned subsidiary of BARRA, Inc. with operational independence

Business Mission: RogersCasey is a research-based global investment services firm committed to delivering value-added consultative services and products that enable institutional investors to exceed their goals in complex and fast-changing market environments.

Client Service: RogersCasey's expertise is in the design, implementation and monitoring of investment programs. A team approach allows clients to access information and issue-solving capabilities firmwide. Each client is assigned a relationship team with accountability for all day-to-day activities. In addition, research specialists have responsibility for coverage of specific asset classes. These specialists are called upon as needed to assist with client assignments.

Assets Represented by Client Category*:

	NUMBER OF CLIENTS	ASSETS (in billions)
Corporate	105	$155
Public	11	100
Foundations & Endowments	10	30
Other	11	30
	137	$315

*As of 7/30/96

Services:

Investment Consulting:
  Defined benefit pension, Endowment, Foundation, Insurance, Hospital, etc.
Defined Contribution:
  Investments, administration and education
Alternative Investments:
  Private markets
Strategic Investments:
  Customized multi-manager programs.

Strong Funds

Strong Capital Management

One Hundred Heritage Reserve, P.O. Box 2936
Milwaukee, WI 53201
Phone: 800-338-9699 • Fax: 414-359-3390

Key Contact:

Rochelle Lamm Wallach, *President*
Strong Advisory Services

The Company: Founded in 1974, Strong Capital Management manages more than $21 billion for over 750,000 individuals and institutions. Strong's nationally recognized mutual funds are 100% no-load. Strong Retirement Plan Services provides a full range of retirement plan services—investment management, daily valuation recordkeeping, plan administration/compliance, and participant education and communications—all with an important distinction. At Strong, we understand that investment performance alone is not enough: you and your employees deserve much more—competence, attention to detail and a can-do approach. In short, outstanding service in everything we do.

Retirement Plan Services:

- Open Architecture investment selection, including Strong Mutual Funds, other well-known mutual funds, a stable value fund and company stock.
- State-of-the-Art Daily Valuation recordkeeping.
- Complete Enrollment Materials and On-Site Educational Workshops delivered by experienced educators and communication specialists.
- Easy-to-Read Participant Statements, including asset allocation models, and 24-hour access to Strong's Automated Telephone Information System.
- Partnership Not Salesmanship. A team of expert retirement plan specialists works with you throughout the life of your plan. Our account managers are attorneys, CPAs or hold graduate business degrees.

Investment Disciplines:

Domestic Equity	International Equity
Domestic Fixed-Income	Cash Management
International Fixed-Income	

Expert plan administration, state-of-the-art recordkeeping, comprehensive employee communications and flexible investment options—all in a one source approach. That's the Strong Advantage.

T. Rowe Price Associates, Inc.

100 East Pratt Street
Baltimore, MD 21202

Key Contacts:

T. Rowe Price Retirement Plan Services, Inc.
(A subsidiary of T. Rowe Price Associates, Inc.)

Charles E. Vieth, *President*	410-345-5763
John R. Rockwell, *SVP, Sales*	410-345-2077

Year Founded: 1937

TRPA Assets Under Management: $89 Billion
(as of 6/30/96)

Special Areas of Expertise:

T. Rowe Price Associates offers a wide range of mutual funds and investment management services to institutional and retail clients. Retirement Plan Services is the subsidiary dedicated to meeting the needs of the defined contribution market. A pioneer in offering mutual funds as retirement options, T. Rowe Price provides investments, plan sponsor services and participant services that can be tailored to meet a client's specific needs.

Investment Approach:

T. Rowe Price's investment approach is based on fundamental research and strict adherence to fund objectives. We seek consistent, strong, risk-adjusted performance.

Plan Sponsor Services:

T. Rowe Price provides plan sponsors with a complete array of recordkeeping and plan-related services. Clients benefit from more than a decade of experience in providing innovative solutions.

Participant Services:

T. Rowe Price has for years been at the forefront of investor education. We are committed to helping participants understand how to plan and invest to achieve a financially secure retirement.

UAM Retirement Plan Services

A Subsidiary of United Asset Management Corporation (UAM)

1133 Avenue of the Americas, 28th Floor
New York, NY 10036

Key Contacts:

Mary Rudie Barneby, *President*	212-730-8500
John Bigley, *VP Sales (Northeast)*	212-377-2474
Marc Brookman, *VP Sales (West)*	714-489-3300
Richard Gray, *VP Sales (Midwest)*	212-377-2473
David Harris, *VP Sales (Southeast)*	404-240-8340

Assets Under Management:
(UAM) $155 Billion

Overview: UAM Retirement Plan Services (UAM RPS), a defined contribution (DC) services provider, is a wholly owned subsidiary of UAM, a publicly traded holding company founded in 1980. UAM owns more than 40 independent investment management firms in the U.S. and abroad. Together these firms manage over $155 billion for more than 6,000 institutional and individual clients.

Profile: UAM RPS offers a fully bundled approach to DC services for plan sponsors and participants. The company is dedicated exclusively to providing premier investment, recordkeeping, trust and employee education services through a "hands-on" approach to client relationships. UAM RPS professionals have an average of 15 years' experience in DC services.

The UAM Retirement Plan Services Program:
As a full-service provider of DC plan services, UAM RPS can provide a complete package, including:

- "Top-tier" institutional investment managers who offer a broad array of investment options ranging from capital preservation funds to special equity products, structured as separate accounts or mutual funds
- Plan design assistance tailored to meet your company's needs
- Low cost, state-of-the-art recordkeeping and administrative capabilities, including daily valuations, plan-specific toll-free voice response systems, fully automated loan processing and quick turnaround on distributions and statements
- Ongoing educational and communication services, including customized multiphase, multimedia programs utilizing written, audio-visual and interactive instructional techniques
- Comprehensive trust and custody services through third-party relationships with two major trust companies.

The Vanguard Group

P. O. Box 2900, Valley Forge, PA 19482

Key Contact: Donald A. Salama, *Principal*
(800) 523-1036, ext. 9704

Managing assets of over $200 billion, offering over 90 diverse mutual funds, and serving the investment needs of more than 3,200 institutions, Vanguard is one of the most trusted names in the investment industry—and the largest pure no-load mutual fund complex in the world.

America's leading companies rely on Vanguard to provide investments and services for defined contribution plans, including recordkeeping and trusteeship, toll-free participant services, lifelong participant education and regulatory reporting services. Vanguard also handles enrollments, contribution administration and other benefits outsourcing.

Industry Leadership: Two decades ago, Vanguard invented the concept of mutual fund indexing. Today, Vanguard offers well over a dozen index funds in an ever-growing range of asset categories.

Three-quarters of Vanguard's assets are in its highly regarded, actively managed funds, under the stewardship of top investment advisers worldwide. Each fund is managed within tightly defined investment objectives, so investors can rest assured their money is being put to work exactly as promised.

Barron's proclaimed Vanguard the #1 performing mutual fund family for 1995—and for the decade 1986-1995. And Vanguard Funds took 37 spots in *Forbes'* August 1996 list of "Best Buys".

The Vanguard Difference: Vanguard's ability to deliver competitive performance is enhanced by its remarkable cost advantage. Vanguard funds boast an average expense ratio that is just one-third of the industry average, according to Lipper Analytical Services, Inc.

Yet, Vanguard doesn't gain this cost advantage by sacrificing service quality or innovation: *Financial World* magazine recently gave Vanguard its Quality Service Index Award for the sixth consecutive time. And in an Institute of Management & Administration (IOMA) survey of plan sponsors, Vanguard was named "Top Bundled Provider".

Through its top-quality investments, services and technology, Vanguard continues to prove that investors do not have to pay more to get more.

Index to Underwriters

Close More Sales with Accurate, Qualified Leads

✓ Target prospects quickly
✓ Increase productivity
✓ Improve marketing efficiency
✓ Improve client communications
✓ Develop relationships
✓ Maintain leadership

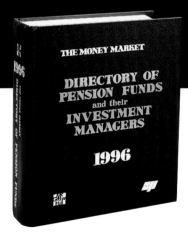

*"The **Money Market Directory** is the most reliable source for marketing information on the U.S. pension market. I have used it extensively for many years and would be lost without it."*

George M. Jamgochian, Senior Vice President, UBS Phillips & Drew International

The 1996 Money Market Directory of Pension Funds and their Investment Managers

The most thoroughly researched reference tool of its kind for 26 years. No other publication presents your marketplace so completely and accurately.

YOUR EMPLOYEES MAY HAVE A FEW QUESTIONS ABOUT THEIR 401(k) PLAN

We Have More Than 100 Answers

I*t's not surprising that plan participants have lots of questions about their 401(k) plan—how it works; what they can expect to withdraw from it and when; how to make the most sensible invest-ments for their specific needs; whether or not they should even enroll.*

*As evidence mounts that employees are not investing early enough, wisely enough or simply **enough**, plan sponsors and administrators have an increasingly urgent obligation to respond by giving their employees a solid basis for making sound decisions about their future.*

That's why this book from Investors Press is so important.

A New Way to Boost Plan Enrollment

Written specifically for plan participants and eligible enrollees, **Building Your Nest Egg With Your 401(k)** gives them the confidence and knowledge they need to manage their 401(k). Exhaustively researched by its distinguished author Lynn Brenner—personal finance columnist for *Newsday*, a Times Mirror publication with more than a million readers—**Nest Egg** draws on Brenner's extensive experience and the results of interviews with more than 100 large and mid-range plan sponsors and administrators. In concise, *easy to understand* language, this important new book answers more than a hundred of the most commonly asked employee questions about 401(k)s. These inde-pendent, objective responses will help

your employees make more informed judgments about the value of enrolling early, the maximum amount they should save and which investment vehicles will best help them meet their specific needs and expectations. Throughout this handsome book's 160 pages of text and 4-color tables, charts and graphs illus-trate and explain key aspects of saving and investing. *Easy to understand*, thorough and entirely relevant to participant's practical needs, **Building Your Nest Egg With Your 401(k)** is also an ideal way for plan sponsors to comply with 404(c) voluntary guidelines and provide the impartial, third-party informa-tion participants need as they plan for a secure retirement.

INVESTMENT MANAGEMENT SERIES